Y0-BZT-930

MAKENA'S SHADOW

MONICA K.K. LEE

A Hoku Book
Makali'i Productions
Islands of Hawai'i

FIRST HOKU BOOKS EDITION FEBRUARY 2015

For information, ordering, or to reproduce selections from this book, contact: Permissions, Makali'i Productions,
67-1185 Mamalahoa Hwy. D-104 #143 Kamuela, HI 96743

Book and Cover design by the ever talented S.L
Photos © Monica Lee
Printed in the United States of America.

Library of Congress Cataloging-in-Publication Data

Lee, Monica K.K.
Makena's Shadow / Monica K.K. Lee
p.   cm.
ISBN: 978-0-9961328-0-0
1. Hawaii--Fiction   I. Title.

ISBN-13: 978-0-9961328-0-0
ISBN-10: 0996132805

ACKNOWLEDGEMENT

Enormous love and special mahalo to Shane, who believes in the magic even when I'm not sure that I can pull the rabbit out of the hat. 'O ku'u aloha no 'oe a mau loa aku.

10 9 8 7 6 5 4 3 2 1

No ku'u mau keiki, me ke aloha pumehana.
For my children, with the warmth of my love.

MAKENA'S SHADOW

ONE

I'M SUPPOSED TO BE GETTING ready to board the plane right now; in fact, I can hear Mom's pissy voice hissing, "Gabriel Kane Foster!" She's saying my middle name kah-neh in that chalkboard scratching tone that makes me want to run away from, and not towards her. I move my head slightly just to let her know I'm still on this planet but I think it's pretty obvious to anyone with a brain that I don't want to leave. I don't want to go anywhere. Not with her. And I'm sure not going to stand next to her. Not after what she said.

"You evil, hateful little psychopath," are the exact words she used when I reminded her that if they had taken out an insurance policy on us like I suggested a while ago we wouldn't be in this situation in the first place. But I digress. After all, her stink bombs aren't the only reason why I'm dragging donkey.

Makena is.

I'm having a hard time remembering the last thing I said to my older sister. Was it, "I hate your guts," or, "I hope you die,"

1

or both, like I think it might have been? I keep going over it in my head again and again.

I reach down and gather the fabric around the handle of Dad's old army green canvas duffle; a relic he loaned me because they couldn't afford to buy me a carry on of my own. It smells like spoiled yak cheese and when I yank and hoist the bag filled with my clothes, shoes, and Makena's writing journal (yeah, I stole it out of her room while we were packing. It's my brotherly *right* to keep it) up into my arms, it fills my nose and permeates the air around me.

I see the hairy old woman next to me fanning her face and by the way she's tearing into me with her eyeballs I know she thinks the animal issue is coming from one of my orifices but there's nothing I can do about it, no excuses I could possibly give her that would make her believe that it isn't my fault, that sometimes things just happen so I stop and adjust my bag near her head. It sucks carrying it from underneath but as much as I would like to carry the gigantic body bag by its straps, I can't. It broke while Dad was serving in what he and his friends dub, 'the sandbox'; that place the rest of the world calls Afghanistan, that place Dad left us for twice, that place where he became a war disabled veteran.

While waiting for Mom to take the brake off of Dad's wheelchair, I put my bag down on the floor and untangle my ear buds. As I plug them into my ears, my mind shifts back to Makena and I marvel at the fact that it's only been two weeks, yet I can barely remember how tall she was or what her normal, everyday face looked like. I mean, I know the basics because me and Mom share those same features with her: mocha colored hair, warm caramel skin, deep brown almond-shaped eyes and long black eyelashes. I also know that even though I didn't think she was anything special, people always said she was attractive like Mom; unlike me, who everyone always guessed was Mr. Bean's lost love child. I do remember thinking that Kena was shaped like a deformed stick figure, and that her bubblehead wasn't proportionate to the rest of her but my brain must be spazzing because I can't grasp the exactness of my own sister without the help of pictures.

Mom's getting vicious, signaling me with sharp, manicured nails and a sour-looking face which means she expects me to get my bag and remove my buds. I gather the fart bag up again and pluck the left earphone out of my ear; act like I couldn't hear her before, even though nothing is playing in either of them right now. "What's taking you so long? Are you still thinking about that girl, what's her face?"

"Deanna." I mutter. You would think she'd know the name of my girlfriend by now.

"Whatever, Gabriel. You know, you better get your head on straight. Girls like her are like grease burgers. You can pick one up at every corner. Come on, help me get stuff together, let's go!" She snaps. Fearful of her heavy ring covered backhand, I grab whatever I can. The combination of my bag, dad's bag, her bags and her purse feels the way I feel: cumbersome.

My sneakered feet follow Mom's shiny black stilettos and Dad's scuffed up wheels until we reach the line at the gate. Once we near the small cluster of airline workers, reality punches me from behind and takes my heart.

We're moving.

I knew this day was coming; that we were going to have to leave California. Ever since we got *that* letter from the bank, that *thing* Mom and Dad tried to hide, that threatening *piece of paper* me and Makena found on the dining room table, that *generic* note that was probably mailed out to hundreds of people everyday, yet stained with actual parental tears. It was dressed in blood red capitals, demanding to be read, so Kena and I took it on.

The words were barbed with accusations and the letter oozed with the stench of greed. *Pay up,* it said, in legal jargon, *or we will kick you all out on the streets.*

We both knew Mom and Dad were having trouble finding work, that the bills were piling up so high we resorted to auctioning our things off online to try and keep us afloat, so we knew *why* we were leaving, even though the parents told us that they were thinking about moving us all out to our grandparent's estate in Hawaii just to give us all a, 'change of scenery.' I *knew* us leaving was inevitable; I just didn't know this day was going to come so fast.

The boarding line we are waiting in is growing. It's now Mom, Dad, me, and tons of freaky-deaky strangers. We stand united, and wait for the crisp-uniform wearing people who are flying the plane to pass us. I push my ear bud back in place even though my mp3 player is dead. I would rather pretend that it's filling me up with music than have people talk to me. My eyes find the plastic looking carpet and I focus on the pattern of its fibers. *It's not even real.* I tell myself. *It doesn't even feel right.*

We grew up in that peach colored ranch house that the bank was taking away from us, and my parents spent almost everything they earned keeping it nice. We planted infinite memories in the backyard. Our dreams were captured in the walls and the ceilings of our bedrooms, our laughter fluttered aimlessly through the air of the living room, the dining room, the patio, the pool. Mom's horrible health-food cooking, Dad's easy-burnt meals, Makena's microwaved specialties, and my gourmet popcorn scents were singed into the cupboards, the pantry, and the countertops of the kitchen. Our collective sadness permeated the curtain rods and slept in closets where things no one wants to deal with are hidden. Words of anger were spilled carelessly and left to lie like stains in the crevices of the front door, the garage, the hallways, our parent's room, and that space right in front of the bathroom door.

When my parents got *that* letter, our house was already 'on the market' for a year— but Mom and Dad decided to drop the price even lower so they could still 'come out on top' as they put it when they thought no one was listening. But when the real estate guy told Mom and Dad that it was sold and they'd be walking away with nine thousand dollars and some change after fees, I knew the people 'buying' it were actually stealing it out from under us. I may only be thirteen but I'm smart enough to know that we were getting ripped royal.

I'm also smart enough to know that my parents already spent that money. They had to have. I've watched Mom throw all kinds of paper down for packing, shipping, airline tickets, and Makena.

Makena.

My mind shoots back to *that* day.

On *that last day* my sixteen-year-old sister tickled the

space around her short brown hair with those stupid 'air piano fingers' of hers, closed her eyes and belted out some made-up song about us moving like she thought she was Beyonce or something. She stood right in between the cardboard boxes in our crowded living room, all dressed up like a dumb doll, and, wearing enough makeup to cover all of Hollywood, she gospelized our move.

When Makena stopped with the glory be's and hallelujah's, she spouted that us leaving Riverside, California was the answer to her prayers and claimed that moving back to O'ahu was something she wished for ever since she was a little girl. She danced and spun around like a drunken imbecile, while I threw strings of furious sentences at her in hopes she would trip over them. She eventually left in Mom's car to run some errands and left me behind to stew in her celebratory aftermath knowing full well that my life was ending—she knew that the thing me and my bae Deanna had going on was about to come to a rude end; that it was ripping me apart, that I was mad—hold up, wrong word. I was *enraged*.

They said she got into that accident that afternoon because she drove off the road and wrapped Mom's car into a tree while texting, but they don't know that I was the one who caused it.

Me.

I know this because *I* was the one who was texting her when she died.

I've kept this to myself because I know if I told my Mom or my Dad they'd disown me for life without a goodbye, even when I think my reason for texting Makena over and over again was valid.

She shouldn't have been so ready to leave the only home we knew behind; shouldn't have been so happy. She should have cared that we were leaving everything behind— everyone we knew. So I went off; told her a whole bunch of stuff that yeah maybe I shouldn't have said. I really laid into her— let her know what I really thought about her, told her she was weak, dense, friendless, and unpretty (only I said those things in a not so nice way.) But what I really can't get out of my head, what I really wish I could remember are the words I actually said to her face. If I could go back in time and talk to her again, I'd tell her I wasn't serious; I was just being Gabe. I didn't think anything bad that I wished on her would *actually* happen because even though I meant it, I didn't *really* mean it.

Two hours later the three of us: Mom, Dad, and me were at the hospital.

T W O

Everyone in the emergency room was in full panic mode. Something huge and disastrous must have been happening when we got there because people were coming and going through the doors like crazy. EMT's, doctors, nurses from all directions were ripping through the waiting room. With all the confusion, we somehow found our way into the back; I don't think we were even supposed to be in there looking for Makena; maybe nobody noticed us because Dad's in a wheelchair and Mom was dressed like a janitor, but we just kind of slipped past the radar and let ourselves through. A woman in yellow scrubs who reeked of rubbing alcohol pointed in the direction of a room—an actual room, not the phony kind with the shower curtains hanging all around it like the one I got sent to when I had food poisoning once.

I pushed the door open to let my parents in and from

where I was standing I could see my 'big' sister, all banged up, bruised fingers dangling from the sides of the hospital bed. She had an extreme amount of tubes and wires coming out of her skin, and those were all connected to plugs, which ran into different machines behind her. Her swollen face was purple and waxy, and the old decaying hospital gown they tossed over her chest covered her body like a ragged tablecloth. I guessed it was meant to cover her seeing as how they'd ripped off her real clothes to try and save her life.

An E.R. nurse who just happened to be jogging by stopped and grabbed the doorknob. I told her I was there to see my sister and she told me that I couldn't be there, that no one should have let us in (*I have to see her*) that I should stop (*let me see her*) and see her later (*later when?*) that I might be traumatized (*you'll be traumatized if you don't let me in to see her!*) but I shoved her away from the door (*but not hard enough to hurt her*) and plowed my way through the fog to Makena's bed. I didn't want it to be true. Couldn't believe it. Not when she had seemed so normal— normal for Makena anyway— a few hours before. I needed my own eyes to prove it. And even when my own eyes could see it I didn't want to believe it.

I'm squatting on the airport floor now because we've been standing in this airbus boarding line forever. I try to focus on the picture of Makena that Mom has dangling from the outside of her purse but my twisted mind still sees her twiggy arms tied down with I.V. Meds; my memories can't release the sight of the puke green line on the black screen of the machine that was supposed to show every beat of her heart, but was instead telling us that there was no sign of life connected to the other end of its wires. I try to memorize the details of her senior portrait, her oval face, her braces, her thin neck, the mole on her right cheek, because I can't get her purple lips, frozen into a terrified scream, those bruises, those bumps, the blood, and the vacancy in her eyes out of my mind. Worse, the scent of medicine and sterile hospital cleaners seems to follow me around like a ghost. I can't get it out of my skin or my clothes no matter what I do. It just lingers in the air beside me. Hangs on to my fibers like a shadow.

After I saw her like that, I started to laugh uncontrollably. Not because I thought anything was funny, of course it wasn't funny there was nothing funny about it. It's just something my nerve synapses must have told my body to do it all on its own. Laugh and shiver and yell out like some crazy person. I felt like such a scuzzbag. But I couldn't stop.

People wearing cornflower blue scrubs surrounded me. I couldn't tell if they were doctors or nurses at that point, only that they were trying to subdue me and/or Get. Me. The. Hell. Out.

Then Dad started screaming at the doctors, the nurses, Mom, me. I remember him telling me to shut the hell up, accused me of cracking up because I was happy about my sister dying. Said *I was always jealous of her*, because *I* am such a *screw up* and she was damned near perfect. And then he pointed at me and said, no he screeched, "You think this is funny? That it's all a joke? She's not coming back again! She's not coming back! Do you hear me? Do you hear? *It should have been you. It. Should. Have. Been. you!*"

I wish it was you! I think I screamed instead of just internalizing it like I thought I was doing because he tried to

10

attack me with his shoe, then the plastic containers sitting on the table next to my sister's bed, then, the pole that carries and regulates the I.V. Medicines.

Security came and hauled both of us off.

It's been two weeks.

Two whole weeks since the whole Makena thing. Thirteen days of living with a maniacal Mom. Three hundred and thirty six hours of me and Dad and frightful silence.

An airline worker is making gestures to everyone to move toward the pane glass windows. Make way for all the special people to go through, she's saying in airplane talk. The people who are rich enough to buy first class tickets go first. We watch them pass us by and I can't help but notice how pleased with themselves they all look. As they walk past us peasant types, I wonder if any of them works for the bank that wanted to kick us out of our home.

The business class goes next and I'm sure that one of them is the guy at the bank who personally folded the eviction letter and stuffed it in the envelope. Maybe one of them is even the venom hearted jerk who was in charge of choosing the stamp that read, 'LOVE' that sat on the top right hand corner of the tear stained envelope. I'm angry, but calm down once they announce that people with small kids and wheelchairs are up next.

Mom pushes Dad, who hands the lady in uniform our tickets. She rips, smiles, rips, smiles, rips, and directs us down the ramp. We follow the people in front of us until we get to the door of the airplane. Before I step inside, I touch its cold, metallic body and my heart bursts and falls out in droplets from my eyes and nose.

11

The flight attendant notices and rushes to get me something to wipe my face with.

"Are you alright?" She's asking, her soft Asian face filled with concern.

Mom notices and does her best job explaining. She says, "He's under a lot of stress. We're moving, not visiting."

The woman hands me a whole box of tissues and nods. "Don't worry. You'll have a good time there. You're lucky. Lots of people wish they could live in Hawai'i…"

She says Hawaii funny—like Huh-vie-ee but I'm in no mood to correct her. I slide into my seat next to the window and stare out of it. I don't want to talk to her and I really don't want to hear about how lucky she thinks I am.

Dad sees this and apologizes like I'm some kind of dumb animal.

She forgives him and gives me one of those sympathetic smiles, like I care. They don't know me. I'm over being worried about leaving the only home I remember in beautiful, sunny California. So over my bae Deanna with her *hott* blond hair, her *hott* hazel eyes that complimented mine, her *hott* scar-less legs, her *hott* lips that I never did get to kiss (but probably could have if I wanted to.) At this point in time; at this very minute the only this going through my stupid head is: What was the last thing Makena said to me? Why can't I remember things that should be fairly easy to remember? Does everyone who experiences the sudden death of a sister go through this?

THREE

After we take off, the same lady who took away Dad's wheelchair is the same one who winds up bringing Makena back to us. And just to make things clear, I mean Makena's ashes. Not her corpse.

Mom and Dad had her cremated so they could take her everywhere with us.

When Mom told me what cremation was, (reducing the dead to dust) I went and researched more about it. (Did you know that there are whole societies dedicated to cremating remains? Imagine being a member of one of those creepfests.) Anyway, I learned:

1. Cremating takes 2-3 hours in a specially made oven that gets über hot and I mean hot like 2000 degrees hot.

2. It's done in the funeral hall (and in some churches) and all they need is a cardboard box or a wooden framed container to collect the remains.

3. Some people like to view the body and watch it incinerate until all that is left is sandy colored skin dust with chunks of bone and bits of teeth.

4. We could've taken Makena home in a paper bag if we really wanted to. (Not like we would've, but they do give that option to people.)

5. Hawaiian people (which, I guess is us seeing as how Mom's always saying that our ancestors were living on those islands long before anyone else was) don't like cremation because bones are extremely sacred and hold a lot of mana or power, according to this one website I found. Traditional Hawaiians like my Mom's parents even believe that a proper earth burial is better for the soul, which is probably why Grandma is so pissed off at Mom for burning my sister instead of burying her. (I know this because I heard my parents talking about it.)

But even knowing that last part, I thought cremation was an undeniably good choice for us in our situation— I mean, I can't imagine how people would have felt if they had to sit next to Makena's body on the plane.

"You didn't have to check it in." The black-haired airline lady whispers loudly to my Dad, and she hands him the container filled with my sister's cremains. Mom pries it out of his hands and cradles it like it's baby Jesus.

I frown at the dumb thing because I know Makena and that's not the kind of place she would have chosen for her dust to settle. And what makes me aggro is that I even asked my parents to take me with them the day they went out to choose it— I would have picked something nice at least; some kind of genie of the lamp thing with her favorite animal (the dolphin) on it.

But no.

Mom and Dad went by themselves to get Makena's ashes. *They* bought that fugly, plastic, see-through container with the demon-red screw on lid, and had the funeral necroman fill it to the top with skin flakes. It's the very same container that Mom is presently bouncing on her knee as if it were a living, breathing kid and if I described that to you as well as I hope I did, you would know that basically, they bought a clear mayonnaise jar with a plastic cap cover to house the sandy colored remains of my older sister.

Mom's reasoning was, "this is the only thing that made sense. It's safe, and TSA won't question us about it."

They were wrong though, because the army of privatized gatekeepers *did* ask my parents to provide documents. Thankfully, they had this to get all of us through

    :

OBITUARY

Foster.

Makena Nalani Foster born on Easter Sunday, 1998 in Honolulu, Hawaii. She is the daughter of Marcel Kane and Gavin Foster, and the sister of Gabriel Kane Foster. She is also survived by her grandparents, one uncle, two aunts and numerous cousins. No Memorial. No Funeral. No flowers.

While Mom and Dad were cheering because they
accepted the obit, I was celebrating because they didn't force
any of us to taste it like they do to other people who carry excess
body fluids in plastic containers.

꒜ ✵ ꒛

Mom is in the tiny toilet room with the origami door,
the doll sink, and the soap marked, 'tropical breeze' when Dad
rears his goofy looking head towards me. Our eyes lock and for
a minute I think he's about to apologize—he's long overdue for
one because of those nasty things he said to me at the hospital—
but he doesn't say anything that even resembles a sorry. Instead,
he licks his lips like a lizard and mutters, "Man, it's been a long
time. I never thought we'd be heading back to that place again,"
his sky blue eyes sparkle like twin UFO's from a sci-fi movie,
"you know—the place where I met your mom."

I sigh. He finally broke his code of silence but doesn't
even have anything useful to say like *oh gee, Gabe, I'm sorry*.
I'll admit that I kind of want to hear the story of how they met
because I've never actually heard it coming from *his* mouth
before, but really, I'm just looking for a few kind words of
apology. I want one before he continues to try to be my friend,
but he doesn't care. Just keeps yapping.

"We were in Waikiki. You know? And she was staying
over at the hotel where I was working as a bellman because she
had this regatta to race in."

"Wait," I tell him, and sit forward to hear his story. "Mom
was a racer?"

"Yep." Dad says, all frizzy brown hair and coffee stained teeth.

Mom's story was a lot different. She said they met in Waikiki while Dad was working and that they dated for a while afterward but she didn't mention any kind of race— not that I don't believe she would have done something like that—she's always been super competitive with everyone and I mean *everyone*. Makena included. When Kena became a cheerleader, Mom tried to put her uniform on and when it wouldn't fit her right, she had it altered so it would. It looked fine on Mom but when Kena wore it, hobo city. When Makena went to dances, Mom dressed up and went along too. She said she was a chaperone—but do chaperones wear crowns and sashes? Kena didn't think so either. So yeah, I can imagine a thinner her whipping around rubber buoys with her hydroplane or personal watercraft—same ones that were in the water shows we used to go to when she and Dad were making money. I give in and ask Dad, "What'd she race?"

He rubs his right leg. He's been saying he can feel stuff in his legs every once and a while and I wonder if now is one of those times. "Canoes."

I don't see how he can be serious. "Canoes?"

"Yeah. Canoes." He says again. "You know, outrigger canoes with the things, and the thing," his gestures indicate that there are two long 'arms' attached to the boat that leans away from the canoe, and some other long part that was somehow holding on to those arms, so that it laid flat on the water next to the boat. "And oh yeah, the six paddlers, and the fourteen on the right, fourteen on the left, hut-ho type of deal. Canoes."

I settle back in to my usual seat of disappointment. There's no way something like that could go fast. "Uh."

"So yeah, there she was, staying with her friends and her family and her fiance…"

"Mom had a fiance?" I ask, even though I don't know why I did. I'm not naive enough to think that Dad was the only man she'd ever gone out with, especially since Mom was kind of attractive for an old person but like the racing thing, she'd never mentioned a fiance before.

"Yep." Dad says, and uses both hands to adjust his legs. "She had a fiance, and they had a date set; they were going to get married and everything. Her whole family already accepted the dude like he was already one of them and he acted like he belonged to them too." Dad frowned a little, and then went on. "He was all buddy budsky with that big rich family, all tight, but I stole her away from him with my charm."

Charm. I can feel my face changing; morphing, if you will, into a smirk. Thankfully, he doesn't notice it. Just keeps rattling.

"I joined the military, and we ran off and got hitched after you were born. Of course, we wound up in California because it's where I was stationed last, and where I was discharged and I always thought we'd stay there but well, things aren't always the way we want them to be, as you can see." He patted his legs, leaned into me and mumbled as if he thought people were eavesdropping on his one-sided conversation with me, "yeah, we've had our share of money problems but so what? Everyone's got 'em these days, right? Anyway, your grandparents on your mother's side offered us a home to keep—to *keep* now, so that's

19

good. So I guess we're just going to have to try and get along so we can make it work." His eyes went off to some far off place and stayed there for a while.

Mom's freshly made up face is popping out of the tiny toilet cupboard, and even though Dad can't see her, I swear he can smell her because just as she's standing over his shoulder, he says, "if I can say one good thing about Oahu, it would be meeting Marcel. She changed my whole life."

His words are so cliché, I want to tear my ears out. But of course, Mom sinks right into his arms. "Aw, baby…"

"What?" He asks, with raised eyebrows. "It's true."

"I love you." She whispers, tears finding their way down her bronzed chin.

"I love you more." Dad whispers back and hands her Kena-in-a-jar.

I find the airsickness bag in the magazine pouch in front of me, open it up, and wait for the barf to pour out.

The whole airplane ride was five and a half hours. Five and a half hours of listening to my parents whisper weird things to each other, of trying to watch lame movie number two (I fell asleep during lame movie number one) of eating chunks of cardboard labeled 'chicken primavera,' of drinking juice so sweet I swear it was really plain syrup. According to the flight attendant that handed my parents Makena's cremains at the beginning of our flight, we have approximately ten minutes to go before we land.

"Please raise your shades so the people next to you can see out the window," an unknown high-pitched man voice says. I do as I'm told and squint when the light comes in. I see the people in the middle row turning to look out my side, so I lean over and try to see what they're looking at. All I see is water, water, clouds, and clouds.

"Ladies and gentlemen," the mysterious male voice starts again, "we are going to be coming around for the last time to collect the forms you have already filled out that asked you to declare any illegal plants or animals that you may have brought with you. Please hand them back, along with any writing instruments that we may have loaned you and keep in mind that the beautiful islands of Hawai'i are by nature, pest free zones."

He has trouble putting his mic away and we can all hear him cursing himself out over it. On a normal day I would probably have pointed and laughed at the fool but it's not a normal day. It's the first day of a miserable life.

The Asian airplane lady is sweeping through the aisles and collecting everyone's paperwork. She stops next to Dad and tries once again to practice her superior customer service magic on me. Her coal black eyes are caffeine addict wide and her whitened teeth look luminous under her clown red lips. "Smile, in a few seconds you're going to be at home in paradise." I manage to get my lips to spread out across my face not for her amusement, but out of sheer fright. "There you go, now there's a good looking smile." She sings and moves on towards the front of the plane.

I clench my eyes shut and the actual taste of barf hits the back of my throat. I know this is the signal that I have way too much anxiety building up inside of me so I gaze over at my parents hoping that the sight of them will somehow smooth out the rocks in my guts. I want them acknowledge me. To tell me that things are going to be great and I'm going to love the new world that we are almost standing on; even though I'd frown at that response, and even though I know they'll both be lying through their faces at me. But just by eyeballing the two of them I know it isn't going to happen. They're too busy getting stupid with each another to care about me.

I look over at the tragedy that is Makena's new vessel. Even she's turned upside down because of how Mom and Dad are acting and I mean that literally. I don't want to touch the container—she hated when I touched her while she was alive, I couldn't begin to imagine how she'd feel if I tried to touch her while she was dead—but I don't want her spilling out all over the place so I tap Mom's shoulder. "Mom, Makena's flipping out."

"What the hell are you talking about?" Yup. There's the Mom with the sour attitude that I'm used to.

"Makena." I repeat, "Is flipping out of your lap."

"Oh my gosh!" She gasps and reels Makena back into the safety of her arms.

I don't have to shake my head at this point; the airplane is doing it for me. The descent is way rough and even though our neighbors are panicked, I'm not even a little scared of death. After everything that's happened recently, I welcome it.

The fasten seat belt lights pop on with along with the doorbell sound effect and that seems to be the fix. We're flying normal again. Everyone in the middle aisle is stretching over their seats to see out of my window again. I stretch over and look too.

I see some green, some brown, tons of buildings and warehouses, and long black roads reaching to everywhere, each one smothered with cars. It damages the visions of the Hawaii I had in mind; the ones that were filled with pineapple trees, coconut fields, and wide empty beaches covered with white sands. Thanks to television and the movies, I expect to see grass shacks and volcanoes spouting red, fiery lava, not a baby L.A. From what I see, Oahu's just an exotically named island disguised as a modern, every day urban city covered with concrete structures.

But the water— the bright blue of it, the way it sparkles in the midmorning sun, and the way carries the boats around is something completely different than what I'm used to. I try not to be impressed as we, "start our descent to Honolulu International Airport," as the guy who cussed himself out over his microphone a little while ago is so eloquently saying right now, but the closer we get to landing, the more I feel like it won't be so easy to hate something so stinking beautiful.

F O U R

As we're walking down the jet runway that connects the airplane to the airport, I'm amazed at how gross the air feels. My bag-laden arms feel sticky, like I've been sweating to the oldies even though I just spent hours upon eons on a cool airplane.

Walking behind Mom and Dad isn't doing me any good either, since Mom's ultra high heels are making her move slower and more carefully than usual and Dad's wheels are stopping at every bump in the ramp.

I'm roasting in the island's humidity and am starting to feel like, if all the people dawdling in front of us don't kick it up a notch, we'll all be fully cooked before we reach the building. I contemplate moving ahead, just putting my head down and plowing through all the traffic but I know Mom, and she'll have something to say if I start shoving people aside with my noises and my elbows. Instead, I grit my teeth and bare the heat in the slow, s-l-o-w, s—l—o—w line of bodies.

We finally reach the lobby and I feel like I just got out of the shower, only I'm covered in salty body grease and skin oil. Luckily, Dad says he's got to poop, which means I get to sit down again. We find the bathrooms and I plop myself down onto the slick, black leather chairs and wait under the air conditioning vent for my parents. I am the designated bag watcher but you better believe that I am not watching anything right now. My mouth is wide open and thanks to the Chinese finger trap we just emerged from my curly brown hair is slicked back gangster-style with perspiration. Not that I care. I am completely enraptured by the sweet iciness of the air conditioner as it blows across my face, arms and neck.

"Gabriel." My Dad calls. "You sleeping buddy?" *I like that he calls me buddy. Not.* "Wake up, come on. Let's go. Hup-two-three-four."

I open my eyes and shoot him a smile so plastic it could pass for a credit card. He buys it as genuine and pats me on the head. I know he's being affectionate but it makes me feel more like a dog than a kid. I pull away from him and stand up. He's staring at me and it's freaking me out so I tell him, "Flight was good."

"Yup." He says. We agree on something. "Listen bud;" ugh, again with the 'b' word. "I just want you to know that…"

"You ready? Come on, let's get moving." Mom had to interrupt our moment. He was making a breakthrough I swear it. He was about to apologize but she ruined it. Ruined it. "Nalu just texted me. They're outside." They? Uh-oh. She's looking at me with those scary eyes again. "What are you waiting for? Grab the bags, let's go."

As usual, I do as I'm told and I do it cool and calm, like a professional. But as she's fixing her hair I notice something. Makena is gone. "Mom?" I ask.

"What?" She sputters.

"Uh, where's Makena?"

Her face morphs from irritated to horrified in an instant. "Oh my God, oh my God!"

"You shouldn't take the Lord's name in vain," I say, repeating what she's constantly telling other people.

"Oh shut up." She snarls and runs at Dad. "Gavin, do you have her?"

"No." He says, and his hands shoot up in a defensive block. "I thought you did." He thinks fast and squeaks, "did you leave her in the bathroom?"

"What? No!" Mom says and paces. She's trying to remember where she last had her, I can tell. But I know exactly where she is. I drop everything on the shiny leather chairs and run back toward the plane.

No one is at the podium, but the don't-cross barriers are in place. I look out the window at the plane. It's sitting patiently and there are people underneath it fixing things but other than that, there are no other employees to be found. I know we're in a rush so I grab the vinyl snakelike rope, unhook the divider and let it drop to the ground. The metal end crashes against the metal at the base of the stanchion hopefully drawing some attention. I need help and I need it now. Still, no one bothers to talk to me so I cross over the line and book it down the runway.

I get to the bend, and finally see someone standing at the end next to the door of the plane. As I approach the person, I notice that it's the woman— the same one who took Dad's wheelchair, and brought back Makena's cremains. The same woman with the glazed stare and the clown makeup who was all up in my business; the woman I smiled at out of fear. Great. "Hi. Excuse me, ma'am. We—I mean my Mom left some stuff on the plane."

"I'm sorry," she coos, cocking her head to the right. "I don't recall seeing anything. Try calling customer service."

"No—I can't—I can't leave without it. It's important."

"Help!" Mom's voice is behind me and she is screaming like she lost her mind. "Please, oh please don't leave." I blink and she's right beside me. "I'm a terrible parent. I-I-I left my child on the plane."

The Asian woman straightens her head and furrows her brows. "There are no children—your son just got here."

"She's talking about the thing. The thing I was just trying to tell you about. It looks like sand in a mayonnaise bottle." I explain, feeling desperate.

Mom gives me the evil eye. "How dare you say that about your sister."

"Oh," the airline lady yelps and throws her hand over her mouth. "Oh my. Oh my oh my oh my." She runs back into the plane so we follow and watch in horror as she starts digging in a large trash bag near the back.

"You threw her away?" Mom shrieks.

The woman says nothing, just keeps going through the piles of cups and napkins and straws and other miscellaneous junk people left on the plane. She comes up empty handed and runs to another bag on the opposite end of the row.

"How could you throw away my sister?" I yell, trying to get Mom to see that I didn't mean to call Makena 'thing,' I was only trying to help.

She stops, looks all kinds of apologetic and pulls out the jar filled with Makena's ashes. It's covered with three kinds of

27

gum and the black stickiness that dives to the bottom of coffee cups when it gets cold. "I'm so sorry." She says, and hands it over to Mom. She doesn't even bother to wipe it off, just passes it on as-is.

I look at the lady like she's in trouble. Like she'd better prepare herself for the wrath that is about to come her way but Mom simply takes it, cradles it like a small child who found their long lost doll, and cries. She drops down to the nearest seat and pulls her legs up so that her knees are folded and touching her head. It's awkward to watch her like this, and it's making my heart sore but I can't look away.

The Asian woman comes down the aisle and falls to her knees right next to Mom. "I'm sorry. I really am." She pauses, looks over at me like she wants my opinion or some kind of story or explanation but I don't feel like I owe her anything. I didn't throw someone's loved one in the trash, she did. I just glare at her and glance down at her name tag. It reads, 'Donna Harper.' "I feel really bad…" she purrs, hands fixed on her hardened, product covered hair.

"Come on, Mom." I mutter and grab my Mom by her elbow. "Come on." She gets up and lets me guide her down the aisle and out the door. We step out onto the jetty for the third time. It's probably hot. I don't know. I don't care. She's still crying, with both arms wrapped around the stupid jar this time. We catch up to Dad, who is sitting in his wheelchair texting back and forth with who I'd presume is his brother-in-law—an uncle named Nalu who I have never met. Mom collapses in Dad's lap and he gives her a ride to the elevator. I grab everything—my bag, Mom's bags, Dad's bag, and clomp after them. I feel like

Quasimodo meets Frankenstein as I hobble as fast as I can, nearly dropping everything.

My arms feel like they're going to break off by the time we reach the baggage claim area. A group of people who are waiting for their stuff to come out are going on and on about how far and inconvenient everything is here. I frown. People like them take their, 'really far walks' to the escalators and stairs for granted and they complain about having to stand there and wait without even thinking about people like my Dad, who *really* has to go out of his way most of the time to get everywhere yet never complains about it. Maybe they figure because he's sitting it doesn't really bother him—like his arms don't get sore from wheeling himself around. Like he's got loads of time to kill.

I want to throw the bags I have at them but Dad is telling me, "Listen buddy," *again with the B word,* "I know I'm asking a lot of you right now and I promise it'll get better soon but you need to help me out okay?" He pushes Mom's brown hair out of his face so he's not eating it anymore, blows air at it and removes a few strands from his mouth. When he's satisfied, he continues. "I need you to get all the bags from the carousel there when they come out." He gestures to the big silver conveyer surrounded by people. "We'll go wait outside for your Uncle right there."

My eyes follow his index finger. It's like a dungeon. And it's so far away. "What about these bags?" I ask, struggling to hold them.

"You can put 'em out there with us." *Great.* "We'll watch them." *No, you'll watch them. Mom will do what Mom does best, which is fawn over her favorite child.*

Of course, I don't say any of that. I say, "yeah." And put

the bags out front next to a pillar near the side of the road. Okay, so maybe I don't *put* them; maybe I drop them in a clump next to a mean looking old lady but it's not my fault the bags are so heavy.

Dad says, "easy." And shoots me a look that I translate as*, you can't even carry more than twice your bodyweight— I'm embarrassed of you, you little wuss.*

I turn away and head back to the baggage claim.

People there are swarming now and I'm guessing the bags came out. I shuffle my shoes over the freshly waxed floors and glide behind an old lady and some really hott girls. One looks really similar to Deanna—same hairstyle, same height, same build. Mom's voice pops in my head, '*girls like her are like grease burgers. You can pick one up at every corner.*' I catch that one looking so I smile. She rolls her eyes and scowls. "Yeah right." I say. The girls look at me like I'm filth. That move right there tells me Mom's wrong. Girls like Deanna are *not* on every corner.

One by one people leave, lugging bags and boxes behind them. I step forward and claim my space. I spread my legs out wider to show that I have the whole area; that this is my section, it belongs to me. The bags have stopped dropping onto the carousel and I'm looking at each one as they rumble past me. I see Mom's burgundy bag, grab that. Dad's navy blue one, grab that one too. I find Makena's bag—pink, and personalized with colored rainbows in permanent ink. I feel ashamed at the mere sight of it. But it's mine now so I grab it too. I take them and drag them out to be with my parents.

"The boxes." Dad says.

I go back in. I find count them: *one. One big, gigantic box. Two. Two big, gigantic boxes, three. Three big, ginormous, gigantic boxes.* I stack them on top of each other biggest on the bottom and look for one of those guys with the carts. They were all over the place in LA—in fact, that's how we got them on the plane in the first place. But here it's like I'm looking for leprechauns. And it's not like I can go get one myself because you guessed it, there are no carts either. So I push them out the door and onto the pavement. I can hear the one on the bottom ripping, but what am I supposed to do? Pick them up and carry 'em one by one? No way. I keep them stacked and push slower.

Dad's eyeing me out. "Be careful!" What he really wants to say is, *'you idiot, can't you do anything right?'* But he won't say it because we're in public. Trust me, I know. Dad is really anal about his things; his stuff is more important than anything else, it doesn't matter what it is. It could be a piece of paper that is holding his gum, if it's his, he's taking special care of it.

I notice Mom's not sitting on Dad's lap anymore so I look around and see her backside making its way toward a large pickup truck. Dad moves his eyes in her direction, and for the first time since the hospital he looks lost and scared.

An old bronze skinned man is peeking out from behind Mom's shiny brown hair and is waving excitedly. "Hui- ey nay, how you?" He rolls down the window of a lifted, metallic purple flaked truck, (he's got the front seat) and Mom clomps backwards to make room on the sidewalk. His door swings open and he steps out, one worn out blue hued flip-flop at a time. It's the first time I've ever seen anyone from my mother's side of the family in person, and my stomach is contorting itself into little circus performers because I'm looking at the guy I know only from pictures as Grandpa.

He unfolds his body and stands all the way up and my mouth drops open. He's enormous. I'm talking a full foot taller than me. And I'm five foot five. The giant is holding his arms open to Mom and his eyes are sparkling beneath his long gray eyebrows.

"Oh, my beh-beh's back home, I missed you so much I tell you." His tree trunk arms wrap themselves around the middle of her body and he spins her around in full circles the way Mom and Dad did to us when we were little. He stops, puts her down and touches his head and nose to hers. They breathe in and out in sync a few times, and then he steps away from her and wipes the tears from his eyes. "Haunani." He pronounces her name how-nawh-nee and I snicker out loud at the strange name. As far as I know, her name is Marcel. No one I knew has ever called her by any other name.

My mom whispers something into his ear and he turns around and stares at my dad with his eyebrows raised. "Oh hi, howzit. Nice to see you again... uh, Gavin." He walks towards Dad, hunkers down in front of his wheelchair, and reaches his hand out. Dad eagerly takes it. They shake, let go, pause. Then the old man stands up and pats Dad on the head the way Dad pats me: like a dog. "I'm sorry about da girl. An' I sorry about yoah da kine too ah. Yo' legs. You okay?" without waiting for a response, he nods his big burly head. "Good, good." He finally looks over at me, but this time, I want to be the first to say hi.

I walk over to him, hand outstretched. "Hey grandpa."

He looks shocked. "This—this the boy?"

Mom nods. "Yes, Dad. That's Gabriel."

"Wow. He really look like…"

"Yeah Dad. He does." Mom interjects. "And here's Makena." She's drawing all the attention away from me by holding up the stupid mayonnaise jar. I don't even get to squeeze his massive hand. "You want to hold her?"

The old man furrows his eyebrows and gives his head a good sturdy jiggle. "Nah I'm good, I'm good."

A security guard blows hard into his whistle on the road in front of us and the man who I'm supposing is Uncle Nalu pops his horn. I slice through the thick air to try and get the bags into the car. I drop Mom's burgundy baggage, Dad's navy blue luggage, and my— er— my sister's rainbow spectacle in the bed of the truck while everyone stands back and watches. I load the carry-on's that just about ripped my arms apart, and then I dump the boxes. The first two are easy but the last one has a rip in the bottom that is threatening to burst. I make several attempts to lift what has to be the heaviest box in the whole entire universe up over my head but only manage to bang up the back of the truck.

The security guy walks up and shrieks into his whistle once again, and the driver is out of the truck, running over to help me with a scowl. He's not as tall as the old guy but he's a lot scarier looking. Wild black hair, all tangled and bristled, big deep set eyes, palms that look like worn leather gloves, and he's got tattoos, scars, scabs, and muscles everywhere. He's giving me the stink eye, so I know that he already doesn't like me. I back slowly away from his truck with my hands up. He reaches down, lifts the box up from the bottom and tosses it into the back like it was a feather. Then he opens the back door, lifts Dad out of his wheelchair, carries him to the truck as if he were a bag of potatoes and releases him onto the back seat.

"Wow, braddah, you strong," Mom comments in a way I've never heard her speak.

"Nah dat's notting. I dead lift way mo' den dat skinny pencil neck…"

"Nalu." Mom clucks and throws her arms around his neck. "Be good, boy."

The big scary man hugs Mom back for a few seconds, and then pushes her away. He changes victims, looks in my direction, jerks his head upward and raises his eyebrows at the same time. It's not what I'm used to, so I ignore him and extend my right hand out to him instead. He comes back at me with a booming laugh. "What haole?" He tries to grab the attention of the gigantic old man who is working on climbing back into the front seat. "Ho Pops- dis kid for real oh what?" He's right back to me, slapping his rough, weathered hands on my back and pulls me toward him roughly for a brief hug. His face is pushed up against my own, his forehead touching mine, his nose to my nose. I can smell sharp meat in his breath and can't help but pull away a little. I have never been this close to any man, not even my own father. Never been this close to a girl either. I guess he feels the tension between us and lets me go.

"Um, yeah. I'm Gabriel." I stick my right hand out towards him and bite the inside of my lip, waiting for him to introduce himself.

The security guard comes over with his hands on his hips. "Eh, hoy, hoy, you got to go. No parking here you know."

Mom's brother points at the wheelchair and then points

34

at Dad. "Brah. You no can see? We get one cripple in da truck. Geez, have a heart, bu."

The guard backs away. "Oh—okay. But hurry up, yeah?"

I look at Mom's brother. "Wow. That was pretty mean."

Mom's brother's smile is so wide that it shows every single one of his glowing white teeth, including his molars. "For reals yeah?"

I'm confused. He's acting like being mean is a good thing. "Not mean like however it is that you're taking it. Mean as in evil." I fold Dad's wheelchair and lift it into the bed. He sees me struggling. Doesn't help me. It just proves my point.

"Bruddah. You need help."

"Sure." I say, and put the wheelchair down. He's not budging from his spot. Just crossing his arms. I pick the wheelchair up and place my foot on the tire so I can balance Dad's transportation on my thigh.

"Brah. Is dis how you really act?" He's looking over at Mom as if asking for permission to slap me but she isn't paying attention. As usual. "You so prim and proper." His hand drops down and becomes dainty like a girl's.

A little help here would be nice. I would call Mom but she's already in the car with her baby Makena on her lap. I adjust Dad's chair so that it's teetering on the edge of the truck bed. The wheels are right up in my grill so I turn my head and push it in using the side of my face. It falls onto the luggage and settles itself in. "Thanks a lot."

"You welcome, brah. An' by da way, you can call me uncle Bob." He says, chuckling to himself.

Liar. You're Uncle Nalu. "Okay, Uncle Bob." I repeat.

Whatever, creeper. The security guard is back to glare at us again so I open Mom's door and get ready to slide in.

"Bruddah, how old you?" Uncle Creeper climbs into his seat and points his dirty calloused thumb in my direction.

I stare at my parents and growl, "thirteen and a half."

"Chir-teen an one half? You one scrawny little buggah yeah? T'ot you was five. Get in da back—you close to legal." He points at the bed of the truck and I climb in with the rest of stuff. He doesn't even wait for me to get comfortable; he just takes his foot off the brake and starts going. I jerk forward and panic, pushing everything so that I'm in the middle of the mess we brought, sitting on some plywood scraps like a scared rat in a cage.

"Eh," he calls out again through the open window in the back. "No sit on top da bags ah, befoah da Po-po give me one ticket. Stay away from da edges, and hold on; I drive small kine nuts dats why." He turns to my dad and wiggles his eyebrows up and down. "No worry dude, I goin' whip dis kid into one man foah you."

The stoplight turns green and he peels out, leaving me to inhale clouds of black smoke. We're in Hawaii for less than thirty minutes, already I'm miserable.

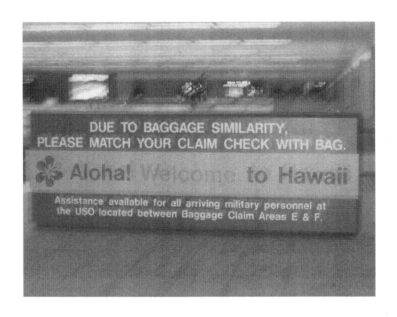

F I V E

The wind is whip-slapping me in the face and I feel like I'm fighting against *the Invisible Man* in a *UFC Octagon*. This is the first time I've ever ridden in the back of a pickup truck, because where I come from *it's illegal* so the experience is definitely an eye-opening one. So eye opening that my eyelids are ready to peel off of my head from the force of the air. Just as I think that they're about to dislodge themselves and fly away alongside the sharp bits of rock and bugs that keep coming at me, a garbage truck passes us and tosses sour smelling papers at me. I duck, and press my body low in the empty space between my parent's bags and the walls of the truck. It's not the ideal ride but at least I stopped Brazilian body wrestling with the air.

It's warmer down here in the center of clutter. Now I know what an egg feels like. I try to get comfortable in my nest, so I scoot towards the empty spot, squash my head to the plastic lining beneath me, and let the circular ridges press into my right cheek. I close my eyes and fold my legs so my knees are exposed to outer space. The truck doesn't like me cuddling with it—it keeps shaking my head off its back but I don't mind. The jostling helps knock the, 'what-if's' loose so they're not stuck in the back of my skull anymore.

The 'what if we were back in California instead of trapped

here, on this island?' Is the first one to come, followed by: 'what if everyone in this family is like Uncle creeper?' and, 'what if we really *do* have to live in a grass shack?' But so far, my favorite 'what if' question of all, is the one about my sister. What if she was still alive? The thought brings her back with me. If Makena was living, she'd be stuck down here in this stupid hole with me and we'd both be hating life as a team. Then we'd probably find something to fight about, and she'd probably snap at me and I'd probably curse her out back and it would continue until we were both pissed off but if she was here at least we would be miserable together.

If she were alive, I'd ask her something like, "what do you think about this hellhole so far?" And she'd probably narrow her eyes at me and churn out some cheesy quotation or corny comeback because she was famous for doing that. Knowing Makena, she'd probably answer with something like, "oh em gee, I love it. I absolutely adore it here. It's everything I dreamed it would be and more." She'd tilt her head this way and that like the dizzy pageant girl she was, and smile so hard that her eyes would cave in. After spinning her brown mop between her fingers around a few times, she might have bounced up and down and smiled like a toothy horse. And she would most likely have said, "Well, do you like it? Don't you have anything to say about this beautiful, whole, new world?"

I would frown and shrug my shoulders. "It isn't home to me."

"Well it is to me." She might've said in that singsong way that would've irked me because I know that would have been true. She always wanted to come here, always talked about

'Hawaii this' and 'Hawaii that,' always referring to it as 'home' even though she grew up in Riverside. The traitor.

And here we are, Mom, dad, me, and Makena only she's at 'home' in a jar. I curl up into a ball and think about how unfair that is. I don't even want to be here, yet here I am, cooking under the Hawaiian sun, getting smacked around by Hawaiian wind, sitting in the back of a pickup truck *in Hawaii* pretty much living out my sister's warped dreams while she's forced to watch it from Heaven.

If she even made it to Heaven. I mean, no offense or disrespect or anything, but my sister wasn't the most saintly person. She did mean things to other people, and had a clique that gossiped nonstop. She never stood up for another person that was being bullied by her friends, never got good grades in school, broke curfew, got arrested for it even, and yet, for some reason, everyone remembered her as a 'good person' once they found out she was dead. Go figure.

I squint up at the bright blue sky and study the temperamental clouds. "Are you up there at all, Makena?" I'm yelling but the words are dragged away to outer space by the vicious air. I challenge the wild gusts and keep hollering. "We're here! What do you think?" As those words come out, the clouds cry all over me. It's bizarre because the sun is still out doing its thing, and out of nowhere, the sky decides to burst. I throw my arms up to save my face for that future photo shoot I'll be having (hey, it could happen) in case they got acid rain here, but as quickly as it came it's gone. Part of me wonders if what just happened was an everyday occurrence, or if my sister actually heard me talking to her and answered my questions by squirting me off with water. It's so something Makena would do. I turn my head to the sky and stick my tongue out to see what she'll do next. Nothing happens. "Ha, typical." I roll over so that the other cheek can get its fill of the pulsating and shut my eyes again.

"There are no dolphins here," I scream and sit up in a panic. It's the weirdest thing to wake yourself up like that but it happened—it really did happen—but this time, my words aren't erased by the breeze. And me, sitting upright with liquid sleep all over my face and a group of hott girls in a car right in front of me only makes it worse. I must have lost track of the time and dozed off because I have no idea where we are now. One minute we're on the freeway and the next… ugh, look at me talking in cliché like Makena.

I look around and try to remember what it was that I was dreaming about in the first place. We're in traffic, stopping and rolling past miles of tall green grass. The group of girls in the car behind me stopped laughing and pointing at me so I check them out for a little bit as we inch on towards a small, quaint little town with little surfboard stores and hole in the wall restaurants. Everyone here is half naked; the men with knee length swim shorts and bare, hairless chests, and the women in tiny bikini tops and those skimpy little bikini bottoms that don't really qualify as thongs, but are closely related to them because they show practically *everything* but crack. People here either haul their surfboards by bicycle (under their arms or on a metal carrier attached to the side of their bikes) or carry multiple surfboards by car.

I'm reading the signs that herald our location but I can't understand the meaning or the pronunciation of the words printed

41

across them. 'Mokuleia,' and 'Waialua' are posted here and there but I still have no idea where in the heck we are until I see one in English.

My brain sends alerts to the rest of me and I snap upward again, this time out of excitement. For the first time since we touched down on volcanic soil, I know where we are. This was the place where movies are made, where TV shows like *Hawaii Five-O* and *Baywatch Hawaii* and *Lost* were filmed and where people from all over the world come to watch the ocean and to be a part of it. I feel electric for the first time.

I hold on to the side of Uncle Creeper's truck oblivious to everything that was going on in my mind a few miles before and look onward as we crawl through the busy roads.

I don't know whose idea it is to turn away from the bustle and into a residential looking area, but I'm glad we made the stop. My body was tired of vibrating. My giant grandfather gets out of the front seat, raises his arms to the sun, stretches straight up, bends right, bends left, and yawns. He looks back at me, grins, pokes his head into the backseat, mumbles something and shuffles his feet to the sidewalk. He pauses to pull his little brown wallet, held shut with a thick rubber band out of his pocket, and disappears into the door.

I look at the sign. It reads: '*Pa'ala'a Kai Bakery.*' I practice saying that word in my head turning the letter 'a' into the 'a is for apple' sound. 'Pa-la?' But what are those apostrophes for? Is it for long vowels? Pay-lay? The old man emerges with four substantial sized boxes. He takes them straight to me, opens one of them and pulls out a flaky pastry. It looks like a rectangular turnover, sprinkled with powdered sugar and covered with a decorative string of thick, milk chocolate. He bites into it and smiles at me. "Pa-ah-lah-ah k-eye get ono kine food. Try."

"How do you say that again?" I blurt out.

He repeats himself slowly, "Pa-a-lah-ah k-eye. Hawaiian words are soft and gentle like one sea breeze, not hard and rude like one stink fut." Grandpa explains. "In Hawaiian A is ah, E is eh, I is ee, O is oh, U is ooh. Den H, K, L, M, N, P, W is he, ke, la, mu, nu, pi, veh."

I'm confused. "W is V here?"

"Sometimes." He says. "Sometimes V sometimes W.

43

Depends on da word."

I point at the words on the box. "So these apostrophes…"

The old mans laughter makes crinkles in his otherwise smooth face. "Not apostrophes. ʻOkina. Glottal stops. Pa ah. La ah."

I notice how he stops and says ah-ah when he gets to those things he says aren't apostrophes but look like apostrophes anyway. I smile to say thanks, open the box, dig a goodie out and nibble on it. Five by four inches of crispy goodness, milk chocolate, homemade vanilla pudding, sugar… before I know it, it's gone.

"Pehea?" He asks. "How?"

"Good." I answer.

"Good, or ono?" He laughs.

"What's ono?"

"Delicious."

I lick the sugar off my lips. "Ono."

"Shhh." He tells me, with a huge smile on his face. "No tell. Secret." He reaches out and tousles my hair in a way that makes me feel like a human. Not a dog.

He gets in the truck and I hold tight to the precious boxes. We pass more half-naked people and drive past a sign that says, 'Haleiwa' where we stop again at a roadside stand. This time, we're in a gravel parking lot with a simple sign above it that reads, '*Anakala's Moa Hulihuli.*' Plumes of thick gray smoke billows high into the air and I inhale the aroma of roasted rotisserie style chicken and sweet wood chips. This time, Mom gets out. "Ooh, smell that huli-huli chicken." She sighs.

'*Mmm. Yeah, smells ono.*' I'm about to say, wanting to

44

impress her with a Hawaiian word because I think that maybe she's talking to me.

She isn't. And she isn't talking to anyone in the car either. She's talking to Makena. She whispers something to the jar, closes the car door and walks away, taking the bottle with her.

I peer into the rear window of the truck and see the men in the car exchanging worried glances. They think she's crazy. I mean, I do too but I don't like the idea of other people thinking of her that way; who cares that they're family.

I climb out of the truck bed and stand in line with her. She takes the arm that has Makena in it and wraps it around me. I shudder at the sight of the ashes—the brown and beige colors mixed with grey. I don't want to see it anymore but it's right there in front of my face, pressed right up against my right shoulder and my future glamorous pecs so I can't help but look. I remember there being something in my cremation research about shards of bone, so I comb through it with my eyes. Nothing.

We move forward with the line, inch toward the meaty scent. My stomach grumbles in response but my head isn't hungry. Not with Makena's crem-nants this close to my mouth.

At the counter under a sign that reads 'huli-huli', Mom asks them to make her five hoo-lee hoo-lee chickens. A lady waiting for her order next to us looks over at Mom and says, "oh, I see you brought your own spices! I didn't know we could do that."

I expect Mom to turn and snap the woman's words to pieces and make her eat them just like she used to, but Mom just stands there and shakes. She tries to give me the 'spice bottle' but I refuse to take it. *I don't want to hold it. You can't make me.*

45

I stand there, frozen. Someone reaches over and takes the bottle away. I turn around and see Mom's brother. He holds it under his huge armpit and pays the cashier. The counter lady hands him some change and he uses some of it to pay for four chicken plates with rice. He throws the change from that into a can marked, 'tips' and walks away with Makena's jar under his armpit. Mom folds her arms and sways side to side. Her face looks as empty as Dad's did when he first came back from Afghanistan. It makes me want to turn around and run.

Just as I'm about to, the chicken lady pushes a cardboard box toward us filled with five white bags of huli-huli's, and another bag stuffed with four Styrofoam plates. I grab the box and leave Mom behind. I'm not worried about her; I can hear her ridiculous heels popping dirt rocks close behind me.

I put the box in the bed of the truck as careful as I can, and get in next to it. I'm starving, and consider sneaking another pastry but I don't. I close my eyes instead and eat through my nostrils. I imagine the old people up front passing the four plates around in the cab, forgetting that I'm a growing boy who needs food if I want to reach the height of the giant of a man who is sitting shotgun behind me. *But it's okay. I'll survive. Maybe.*

As if that's not torture enough, the Uncle who claims his name is not Nalu but Bob drives another block and stops again at a place with a line that stretches out like a caterpillar. The sign in front reads:

He pulls into this dirt parking lot and they all get out. I don't budge.

"Boy." The Uncle says. "Yo' Daddy gotta go shi-shi. Go get his chair."

My Daddy. Shi-shi. I stand, pick my *Dad's* chair up, and lower it to the ground from the bed of the truck. *Mom can do the rest.* I sit back in my spot and close my eyes so I can finish the rest of the chicken particles that are caught in my clothes.

"Boy." The Uncle says again. "How you gonna act?"

"The name's Gabriel." I tell him without opening my eyes. I feel a sharp slap on the right side of my head and my eyes flick right open.

The Uncle is making a fist at me. "Punk. Like dis?"

I shake my head no.

"Den get out."

I climb out on the opposite end of where he is. Stand next to Grandpa. Maybe he'll protect me. He does.

47

"Son-of-a… eh, leave yo' braddah alone, ah?" He yells. "You okay, boy?"

Wait, did he say yo' braddah, or just braddah? I must be tired. I say, "yeah-im-aight" and wonder if he even knows my name.

"Go help yo' Daddy, yeah?" The old guy purrs at me. *Again with the Daddy.* To my Mom's brother, he rumbles, "go save one spot in line."

The mean Uncle walks to the end of the line; I help Dad. Open chair, check. Secure the locks that hold everything together, check. Push the wheelchair to the door, check. Parking brake on, check. Help him down, check.

Dad says, "I need to make number two." I look at Mom as her husband gets settled in. She's caressing the jar again. *Why do I bother?* I'm assuming I have to be the one to take Dad to the can. I do that too. I turn him around and pull him up the wooden stairs. He helps me by pulling his wheels towards me. We work together without saying a single grunt.

I wait outside and let him do his business. He's talking to me from the other side of the door about how good the dessert is here. How they're not called snow cones but 'shave ice.' How this place is famous. I listen, but I am paying more attention to a group of girls practicing their cheers. Clap, clap, head tilt, clap, clap, yay. My legs are sore from standing so long I fold them up and squat down against the wall and wait.

I hear the squeal of the toilet paper holder, some wiping, more squeaks, some more wiping, a flush and Dad getting himself on his chair. I stay where I am and wait for him to wash his hands. "Ready." He says, emerging from the room. I hold the door for him, and help him down the stairs. We work together again, no words, no instructions, just two people with a single goal in mind: to get away from there so we don't have to be alone with each other anymore.

We find our way to the others. Fortunately for us, Mom, Grandpa and that man who happens to be related to them are close to the front so we're not stuck searing in the heat like a bunch of meatballs. Unfortunately, we are so close to the front we have to decide what we want, and we have to decide right now. Also unfortunate: the people standing in back of us in line think we're cutting in front of them. Their murmurs are getting louder and louder the longer we stay planted there.

"So stupid." I can hear them say. "Who do they think they are?"

I tell Mom that I think people are upset because we sort of cut; she acts like I'm nuts. But I know what I'm talking about. My spidey senses may not be as keen as I wish they were, which is why Mom's brother was able to smack my head outside, but my auditory sense works. My ears were working perfectly all those times Makena would sneak in half past midnight smelling like trouble and looking a mess. Working fine when Makena would sneak all kinds of random guys into her bedroom window. They were working fine even when my parent's weren't and they're working perfectly now. "That's how *they* are." The people behind us say.

They? I wonder what they have against handicapped people. I stare at the flavor choices: lemon, cherry, grape, pineapple, strawberry, vanilla, a group of things I don't even know and can't pronounce like lilikoi and li hing, and some things that sound horrible as flavors like sour apple, blackberry, and coconut. A really hott girl with black hair is coming near us with a black permanent pen. "Holder?" She asks Grandpa. He nods. "Ice cream?" He nods again. *That sounds pretty weird.* "Beans?" Blech. Again with the nod. "For all?" *No!* Grandpa says yup. *But I don't want the magical fruit; seriously, I don't even like beans in my dinner why would I want them in my dessert?*

The hott girl does a head count, pulls one tall plastic cup with flower petal edges out of a stand for each of us. She asks Uncle who-cares what he wants. He orders a shave ice with two flavors. *Wait, we can get more than one flavor?* She writes it on a white paper cup with a point at the bottom. She asks Grandpa. *He got three flavors. Can I get more than three?* Next Dad, *just vanilla. So predictable.* Mom is mango, strawberry, li-hing *there's that word again. What the heck's a li hing and why would she want it with mango and strawberry?* Black haired beauty turns to me and stares; pen just a millimeter away from the paper cup.

"Uh…" I'm looking. She's waiting. The pissed off people behind me are grumbling about what an idiot I am. I look up and read aloud the first thing I see. "Melona." *What's a melona?* She writes it down. In permanent ink. I'm stuck with that, whatever that is. "Uh, vanilla." *Vanilla! No! Why? You are nothing like your Dad do you understand?* "Uh can I change that one?" I say. She stares at me, at the pen, at the big 'V' mark she just made with ink that will never go away. "Never mind." I say. I look up at the board and decide to go crazy and order a flavor that for all I know could be a type of catfish or something—you know, just to even things out—just to prove that I am unpredictable. "And give me that Lit-chee."

"You mean lye-chee." She snaps, and marks a symbol next to the other letters. I get a brief glimpse of the code that looks so secret that even I, as smart as I am, cannot break it. She turns around and hands it off to a short, bug-eyed girl with oily skin and pimples so white they look ready to burst, and moves on to her next victim. The bug-eyed girl scoops vanilla ice cream *oh the irony*, in each one and tops it with a spoonful of black, runny looking gunk. *Yep, different and unpredictable, that's me.* When ol' bug-eyes is done with her duty, she runs it over to the ice block people.

The ice block people are the workers who are responsible for turning blocked squares of ice into mini white flakes. With clear plastic gloves, they turn and pat the bits of frozen water into the pointy paper cups that are written on, making sure that they are directly under the mouth of the machine when they do it.

They act with precision, never removing their hands until they shape a ball of ice that is as high as the cup itself. Then these guys turn around and hand it off to others who can descramble the markings on the sides of the cups and grab the right flavors. Those people douse the ice with stripes of green, blue, red, and yellow, slip them in a plastic flower cup and call the flavors out while everyone stares. "Lime, banana, cherry... raspberry, mint, green tea." You get the picture. Then it's off to the side. Curious eyes follow the customers who grab their 'shave ice' and we all judge each and every one of them by what they chose.

I wait and listen while they call on us one by one. My entire family collects their shave ice, leaving me to stand alone like-- the cheese. Doesn't matter. I get to snicker at all the guys who get pink cups. *Makena used to say pink was for panty liners.* "Melona, vanilla, lychee." A guy says and slips it into a pink cup. *Damn you, Makena I know you were behind this.* I accept my shave ice and am directed to a counter top height table with wooden spoons, straws and napkins on top of it. I grab two of everything just in case and exit the store. *Whoa, the line got longer.* I look for everyone else who already left me behind and join them. There's no room on the long benches in front of the store, so we're all just sort of standing around teasing the people in the line with our goods.

Mom's brother sees a guy eyeing out his shave ice. He must be scared he's going to get jacked for it because it's festering out and the line isn't getting any shorter, so he prompts us to move toward the end of the line so no one will bother 'us' anymore. This move takes us right next to the garbage can, which is full of loud, swarming wasps. Normally, I'm afraid of insects that sting or bite but this thing— this cold, colorful, delightful *thing* I have in my hands looks too good for me to wuss out over a couple of flying bugs.

A fat chunk of ice from my cup falls and hits my knee on its way down to my feet, so I work hard to save the rest of my dessert from committing suicide and shovel a spoonful of colors into my mouth. *Oh my God—sorry Mom for taking the Lord's name in vain—but this stuff is so goo-oo-oo-oo-ood.* Melona tastes just like a honeydew melon, vanilla tastes like artificial vanilla candy, and lychee tastes like snozzberries. Just kidding. It doesn't taste like anything I'm used to—its sort of sweet and sour not in a Chinese canton sauce kind of way but more like a Granny Smith apple pie without tasting like a Granny Smith apple pie kind of way. I chip away at the top, make a little hole in it and scoop out some creamy white and slimy black stuff. *It's now or never.* It goes in my mouth. My brain says I should be throwing up at the thought of eating beans and ice cream, but my taste buds are screaming, 'you better not interrupt this party we're having by barfing all over us!' *Sorry, Deanna. I'm in love and it ain't with you.*

I stop eating for half a second and stare at my parents. Dad is concentrating hard on carving his shave ice back into a block of ice while Mom is feeding scoops of her rainbow dessert to Makena. Just kidding. *Whoo this sugar is good.* But I bet if Mom *could* feed the remnants of my sister without people looking at her like she was cuckoo-crazy, she would. I'm pretty sure of it.

We get to the truck and Grandpa hands me a chicken plate of my very own. At least *he* didn't forget about me. "Wow." I say, and turn around to watch him let himself into the front seat. He closes the door and grabs the plate Mom is passing to him. Dad moves his head so Mom's brother can stare out of the back window at me. I turn away so I don't have to look at his porky face while he backs out of our parking stall.

We don't wait at the driveway of the overflowing parking lot for very long. Shakas—those hand gestures surfers do where the thumb and pinky are left sticking out while the rest of the fingers are tucked in towards the palm—are exchanged in all directions as people let us out, and we ease out into traffic.

We pass a few more surf stores, gift dust clouds to all kinds of tourists from all kinds of places, and go over a big white bridge with the name 'Anahulu' on it. A bunch of kids are hanging out between the arches and casting fishing rods off the sides of the bridge. I look beyond them and see the ocean, all calm and quiet.

We inch a little further down the road and there are people standing up on surfboards in calm water. Some of them are having trouble balancing but others are pretty good. All of them are holding long black oars and are either scooting along or flipping over. On the sand near a couple of coconut trees I see a group of weird boats that are obviously the kinds of canoes Dad was talking to me about on the airplane. They are long and skinny, with two sideway arms—one in front and one in back that reach toward a skinny floater piece about as long as the boat. My curiosity is piqued, and I am now up on my knees looking past the passing cars and out over a short rock wall. At this point, there could have been a hundred and fifty half naked girls with bikini bottoms that look like thongs but aren't called thongs, and I wouldn't care. Not when I can see for myself what Dad described in his conversation with himself earlier.

We make our way a little further down the road and I see a photographer taking pictures of two really nice girls. Okay, so maybe I lied about not caring about girls in skimpy things. I stare and stare until they aren't visible anymore and then I close my eyes until they disappear from my mind too.

With nothing around but cars and trees for me to look at, I decide to eat. I open my Styrofoam plate and grab the fork that's sitting on the wax paper that they used to cover the food. I peel the paper away and hold the plate to my face, inhaling the smoky aroma. My stomach must not be satisfied with the sugary stuff we just ate because it's rudely trying to get me to throw up.

I dig my fork into the tender chicken thigh and watch the clear chicken juice flow out. The meat is so soft it falls off of the bone and drapes itself over my fork when I poke at it. I take a medium-sized chunk and drop it between my teeth. It has a light hickory flavor, sort of like barbecue but without the BBQ sauce and the burnt parts. Combine the juiciness of the chicken with the sticky, fluffy white rice and you have nothing left but bones, cartilage and those weird stringy gray things that I'm sure are veins or nerve parts. I'm guessing seven seconds is what it took me to finish it. Give or take a few minutes.

We stop again. I don't know what's causing the traffic but everyone behind us now is either staring off into the water with regular eyes or binoculars. I look in that direction too, and see a surfer that was up and riding a wave tumble and fall face first into the white foam. His board pops out first, followed by his head and his body. Then the board and the man spin over each other again and again; both look like they're fighting to be on top.

"Holy Jesus," *good thing Mom didn't hear the scrawny, sunburned guy standing near the truck say that*. "Did you see that? Dude just ate it."

Right when he says, 'ate it', Makena enters my mind. I smile to myself like some weird freak as I recall my dumb sister pouring half a box of iodized table salt into a full glass of water and mixing it with a spoon. "This is what the ocean tastes like." She swore to me. Mom and Dad never took us to the ocean but she claimed she had been before so I believed her. She swirled her thick concoction around with the spoon she found on the floor and whispered, "eat it." Her mouth opened as she shoveled the clear liquid into my mouth using said spoon. I don't know exactly how old we were—maybe I was five and she was eight—who knows. But I do remember it being the consistency of fart putty and that it tasted bad. Really bad. I also know that it burned going down so I spit it out into my hand and wiped it all over her. Then she chased me around the house with the cup threatening to pour all of it over my head. Lucky for me Mom stopped her by yelling that the two of us were going to be *so, so, so* sorry if we didn't cut it out. Because once Dad found out… that was always her threat: *once Dad finds out.* What she didn't know is that we knew Dad was a million miles away and that if he ever did find out there wasn't a thing he could do about it anyway.

I watch now as palm trees, pines, and houses flicker past us on both sides of the street. We slow down to a stop again, find ourselves next to a fierce crowd of people who are gathered up next to the part of the road that is perched on what looks like the watchtower of the sea. I lean over, and spy a huge, mole shaped rock in the ocean. Hundreds of people are standing on it and jumping off into huge, pounding waves. We pass the laughter, the car stereo music, the little kids crying about whatever it is little kids cry about, and creep forward until we reach a sign that reads: 'Waimea.'

My heart does one of those hop-skippity things. That's the beach my sister said she wanted to visit. Ever since we were told that we were moving here, she said it was one of those places she *had* to go. I think one of her poser friends back home told her about it—said it was where all the pro's go and she was really into surfers so she went on and on about it. I turn and peek into the cab. I think about tapping on the window to ask the parents whether or not they remember Makena using the word Waimea every other syllable when we were packing, but they're having one of those conversations that involves a lot of wild gestures and fast moving lips so I spin back around. Mom would fly off her broom handle if I went and interrupted them in the middle of something that looks important but is probably really dumb. And besides. I doubt my parents would remember anyway. Ever since Dad came back from the war it's been all about him.

Don't get me wrong; it's what my sis and me always hoped for— to have Dad home. No more going away to other countries, no more training, no more worries, just him, with us. When we heard he was coming back because of his accident, me and Makena told Mom we'd help take care of him. We were just glad to have him around. But when he did come back, it turned out that we were just really happy about the idea of having a 'normal' family again because Dad wasn't a real Dad and it's not because he had a spinal injury or was stuck in a wheelchair or none of that; he was just… silent. Aside for going out to do his physical therapy he kept to himself, cried out a lot in his sleep; it took some time to get used to.

And him being like that stressed Mom out and then Mom started dragging him to therapy so they could talk about their marriage, and Makena and me were kind of stuck to deal with each other. It sucked. We fought a lot but somehow, we always worked stuff out. Most of the time, she was the villain and I was the buffer. She'd do something bad and I'd take all the hits but I can't complain because I'd just hang a little piece of blackmail over her head and she'd do all my chores so I wouldn't tell. I want to think we had kind of an 'us against them' thing going on. Now, it's just them against me.

You suck, Makena.

We pass a busy grocery store on the corner.

Climb up a steep spiraling mountain.

You weren't supposed to die.

58

My heart pounds as I realize that we must be near. We're closing in on our new home.

You're supposed to be sitting right here with me.

Suddenly I panic.

What if no one here likes me?

I look for a place to escape, but I'm crammed in the back of a pickup truck with tons of baggage all around. There's nowhere to go.

I'm all alone.

We approach an electric gate, which responds to Uncle creeper's gate opener. It creaks open.

Who's going to do my chores now?

S I X

If I hadn't seen how close the other houses were to each other on the way here, I would tell you that my grandparent's home doesn't rest on a whole lot of land but since I did make a note of the houses, I'd have to say that the place they have is enormous.

Their driveway reminds me of a fat caterpillar; we travel along its long upper body toward its curled tail, and pass pathways that lead to smaller houses. There are trails leading to the right and the left that branch outwards to an area beyond what I can see. Mom's brother drives into a neat carport with shelves and cupboards on either side, and we all get out.

I unload Dad's wheelchair, open it, set it all up, hold it still so he can get on, and then pull all of our things from the back. I wait for someone to tell me where to put our stuff. They don't. They're too busy pointing here and there at trees, at fences, at sidewalks, at the house. I move my parent's luggage, my fart bag, and the cardboard boxes to the outside corner of the garage and leave them there, then take the box filled with bags of huli-huli chicken and place it on a tall rock near the porch.

As if he can smell the meat through the door, a boy about Makena's age appears, and without looking at me, grabs the box of food and disappears in the house.

Grandpa grips Mom's hand, holds on to it like he's scared she's going to bolt from him, and guides her towards the house. Dad stops me from going on ahead and makes me push him up the walkway. We pass two burgundy statues on either side of the path that look like dogs but could be dragons.

The fierce looking one is standing on some kind of round container, *oh look, it's Mom and Makena*. The smiling one is stepping on its child. *And there's Dad looking all pleased with himself and me, smashed under his boot of oppression.*

My chest hurts as each step takes us closer. I wonder what my grandmother looks like. *Hey, I really don't know; I have nothing but pictures to go by and they're all really, really old so cut me some slack.* I wonder because in the photos I've seen Grandma looks like a fat, stocky, stern-looking lady and Grandpa is just some short, balding, pudgy man, but now that he's in front of me, I know he's so beyond that; a giant man with giant amounts of kindness. *I hope Grandma is just as nice.*

Grandpa turns around and grins at me. I look the other way and allow the smile to attach itself to Dad instead. I figure, he probably needs it more than I do. I can see Dad's ears move backwards and the sides of his face stretching so I know he's smiling back at the old man. And even though I know Grandpa's smile wasn't meant for Dad, I feel better knowing that it went to the right person. My eyes move back to Grandpa who somehow managed to get a hold of the jar-o-Makena.

"Ready?" He's asking Mom. She nods. He steps backwards out of his flip-flops and uses his huge feet to gently guide them out of the way.

While this is happening, Mom's brother pushes in front of everyone, holds the door wide open, and we are all exposed to what looks like a really fancy restaurant. The floors are dark wood; shiny, and chocolate colored. To the left of the foyer is a rock wall. Dainty ferns and white flowers peek out at us from watery places between rocky crevices while a light trickling waterfall crawls down the side and spills into a trough, which looks like it's cycling water into and out of an enormous tank filled with colorful red, orange and yellow fish. The tank is as wide and as tall as a regular house window, and it's sitting on a built-in cabinet made out of black rock. It must not be actual rock because there are concrete shelves underneath. The top shelf is lined with picture frames holding paper faces, and the bottom shelf is carrying a huge chunk of purple amethyst *to attract wealth*, a jade figurine in the shape of a heart *to attract health*, and other crystals in what I'm assuming is a clear crystal bowl. *I only know all about this weird stuff because Deanna was into New Age things and it made her happy to force me to learn about it.*

To the extreme right of the doorway, is a large gong on a tall wooden stand. A stick with a fabric ball tied to the end of it hangs on a cradle at its side, and without thinking about the consequences I run over and bang on it. I drop the stick as soon as I do. The sound is louder than I expect but I must say, the gong has really good reverb and actually sounds kind of nice bouncing against the walls and ceiling of the house.

"Gabriel Kaw-nay Fos— what the—what's come over you?" Dad growls while Mom's sharp eyes puncture through my skin.

Grandpa only laughs as a tall, slender woman comes running. She's dressed in a pair of short plaid shorts and a yellow tank top, and has long brown hair that looks like a lady on a shampoo commercial. I'm guessing she's an Aunt. "You rang?" She asks me, her voice as melodious as the gong.

"Yeah, s-s-s-sorry." I say. "I couldn't stop myself."

"No, no, no. That's what its there for, to clear the bad stuff out of the house and to call the good energy in." She

63

reaches out and grabs me, and I notice that she's the same height as Mom. *Definitely an aunt.* "Oh Gabriel. Gabriel Kane." *Huh. When she says ka-neh it makes me want to run straight into her arms. Never thought I'd hear anyone say my name like that.* The lady has her paws all over me now, pushing on my hair, rubbing my shoulders, my back, squeezing each side of my face. "It's so nice to finally see you again." She turns her excitement Mom's way and kisses me right in the middle of my forehead. "Oh, I love you, I love you!"

She backs off of me and heads over to Mom. The air around the two of them seems cold. She doesn't say anything to Mom, just grabs her and hugs for a long, long time. She holds until the room grows warm. Holds her 'til tears roll down both of their cheeks, until both of them fall down to their knees weeping for lost causes.

"I'm sorry Mama." Mom mumbles.

Mama?

The woman who I thought was Mom's sister shakes her head, covers her mouth and nose with her long, dainty fingers. "It's okay, baby." She manages after a sob. "It's okay." She gets up, glares at Dad and then finally offers him her hand to shake.

He takes it, holds it between both his hands, and bows his head. "I'm sorry too." He whispers. "Sorry it's taken so long…" he's not letting go of her hand, just holding it and if I know Dad, his hands are wet and clammy around her neatly manicured ones. "Listen, I just want to thank you both so much. I appreciate—we appreciate everything you're doing for us."

Grandma fishes her hands out and wipes them off on his back. Then she turns all of her attention back to Mom. Grandpa must have given Makena back to Mom and left with all the commotion, because she's just standing there alone, cradling the jar like a kid on show-and-tell day. "Oh, Haunani. I'm so sorry about your hi-a-po. Au-we, yeah?" They take each other's hands and disappear into the house leaving Dad and me behind.

Since nowhere in Makena's name is the word, 'hi-a-po' I take it to mean something like 'oldest child' or 'daughter' or something. Dad's making sure I'm not comfortable by not saying one word to me so I ignore Dad right back and look past the foyer to yet another less formal entry where a tall round table with curly legs stands. A long, dark colored rug protects the table's feet, and a tall vase filled with fresh roses—red and yellow— top the table off. Above that, a crystal chandelier (that isn't on because there are so many windows that are bringing in sun) is showering the floor and creamy walls with tiny rainbows. I creep in closer and see a formal living room on the left side and a sitting area filled with board games and bookshelves on the right.

"A-o-le!" A sharp voice yelps, and I swear I get so much air I could dunk a basketball. "No. What you think dis is? Da mainland?" It's my Uncle again. He rushes towards me and points at a little sign shaped like a turtle posted by the door that reads: '*Take off your slippahs- an' no trading 'em in fo' bettah ones when you leave.*' I have no idea what slippahs are but judging by the picture I'm guessing it's anything you wear on your feet. I slide both my socks and shoes off and drop them outside the door.

"Bettah go rinse your feet off first, haole boy- da buggahs is hau-na. Stink!" He directs me towards the water hose and I stare dumbly at my dad, who's still sitting near the waterfall, pretending I don't exist. I clear my throat. I figure, if anyone can save me from this rotten uncle, I know it's him. I wait for him to tell Mom's brother off the way he did to me that day in the hospital when I last saw Makena but he doesn't. The only sound coming from him is the one coming from his wheels as he guides himself away from me and to the places I wanted to explore.

I exit and find the faucet near the dog standing on its baby by the front door. I twist the spigot and feel the comfortable cold dribble down my toes. Unlike home, the water is clear so I cup some in my hand and smell it. Doesn't smell like chlorine or chemicals, so I drink. It's so refreshing I take another handful. And another.

"Are you Gabriel?" A short thin girl who looks about my age taps me on my shoulder. I shoot up. She's built just like Makena was— like a twig. But she's browner with long black hair and smaller, sparkly brown eyes. I nod, 'yes' to her question. She raises her pointy eyebrow and chimes, "Grandma says to come inside so we can eat."

I turn the spigot. It shoots more water—most of it on her shorts. If I didn't know what happened, I would have thought she needed to wear diapers. *Righty tighty, lefty loosey.* "Sorry." I tell her, twisting right as fast as I can but she shrugs it off and leads me back to the front door. She wipes her feet on the mat before walking in, and I copy. I follow her in past the round table with its flowers and rainbows, past the cozy looking living room area, and into a big dining room. In the center of the room is a really long table and on that table are about thirty place settings. Around the table is a mix of benches and chairs and standing behind these are about as many family members grinning at me.

I shoot a weak smile back because I don't know any of these people. I put my head down a little and peer around for the faces I do know. Grandpa and Grandma are standing near the head of the table. To the side of them is a room with a pocket door that leads to a prep room. "What's that room?" I ask the girl who led me in.

"Butler's pantry." She whispers back. "Shh."

The mean Uncle is holding hands with a short, tubby woman who looks a lot older than he is. She's giving me one of those tight-lipped smirks that don't mean much. I should know because it's probably identical to the one I gave to everyone else when I first walked in. Now I know how they all felt when I was giving it to them. I look away from her and find my parents. Mom is on Dad's lap. She's sitting forward, which means that Makena is probably right between them. Neither of them are looking at me.

Grandma's voice slices through the silence. "E pu-le ka-kou." The girl that brought me in hits my hand and we touch fingers. I touch fingers with the boy next to me and we bow our heads while grandma prays. "E ko ma-kou ma-kua," she starts. I try hard not to laugh. I have no idea what any of it means, but it reminds me of a goofy song I once heard called, 'a-wicky-wacky-hula-to-you' "No ka mea, nou ke au-puni," she says, and the laughter expels from my lungs on its own. I snicker and get sharp elbows in my side from both the boy and girl who are next to me.

"Dear God," Grandma continues, "ma-ha-lo for bringing my daughter Haunani and her o-ha-na back to us after all these years." My eyes are closed but I'm smiling. *They sure like to use a lot of Hawaiian words. Isn't this America? Don't they speak English here?* The sound of water is building up inside Grandma's throat. "I am so thankful that we are given this chance to forgive each other," *wow her English is perfect. I guess they really do speak the language here. Wait— can she read my mind?* "And that we are able to hold our Gabriel once again." My eyes pop open. *You held me before?* "I thank you Lord, for listening to our prayers, for making all of this possible. Thank you for our children, for our health, and for the bounty that is before us. Amen." She's finished so we all drop hands and form a line to grab the grub in the kitchen.

I take my place behind the little kids and eyeball the goodies. I'm next to grab a plate but before I get a chance to pounce on the spread that is laid out on the ridiculously long granite countertop in the kitchen, I'm yanked aside by my Grandma and presented to four cousins, two boys and two girls who are all about my age. One of the girls is the one who invited me inside, and one of the boys is the one who I touched fingernails with during the prayer, but the other two are new to me. "Here, meet your cousins. You're all about the same age. Ku-ka ku-ka. Talk. Get to know each other." She tells us, and then floats on by leaving traces of her flowery perfume behind.

We're silent. The line is moving on without me. Food is disappearing from their home plates at an alarming rate. So I go, "Hi. I'm Gabe." And stick out my right fist. *Bump me somebody. Bump me.* I'm left hanging.

The boys glance at each other and then focus their dull brown eyes on me. The taller of the two pushes his loose black curls away from his forehead and lifts his eyebrows. "I'm George and dis is my braddah Joe-Joe." His head tilts towards the wiry boy with braces who lost his concentration and is now thwacking a paper plate against his palm and ignoring me completely. He looks just like George except his hair is straight. "Ovah dea playing wit' her phone is Miriam," his thumb flies out toward a small, shrimpy little girl who looks like she's about twelve years old. She stares at me and rolls her eyes. Goes back to scrolling through pictures of catz on her lifeline. The other girl who told me to come back in is doing the same thing. Scrolling, typing, silently laughing. "And that thing over there is Joella but we call her U'i." He pronounced her name 'ooh-ee' and I start laughing. Not because of her Hawaiian name but because of her 'American' one.

Joe-Joe drops his plate on the floor and lifts both of his arms up in the air. "Ho what, haole? You get one problem wit' her name?"

I shake my head.

"Then why you laughing for? Huh, fool?" He's pulling his long curls out of his face and I can feel the burn coming from his searing eyes.

"It sounds goofy." *There. I said it.*

"What da eff you said?" He bumps his chest into mine. I can feel him breathing on me. His face is in my face, eyes only inches away. "I heard you laughing when Grams was reciting her prayer too, ah. Disrespectful punk."

Some of the little kids run out of the kitchen yelling, "a-ha-na! A-ha-na!"

I back away from him a little. I don't feel like getting into a fight. I'm only an eighth of the way through my How-to be like Chuck Norris video. "Man, what's your problem?"

"What's my—what's *my* problem?" Joe-Joe says and shoves me in the chest with two hands. I fall back onto the floor, hit my back against the kitchen door.

Grandma comes flying in. "Whoa-whoa-whoa-whoa-whoa." She says, hands up in the air. She steps in front of me and grabs Joe-Joe by the ear. "What the heck is going on in here? What are you kids doing?"

Joe-Joe scrunches his face up and tries to take back his ear. It's not working. Grandma's grip is tight. And so are her lips as she talks through them. "What happened? Huh? Joe-Joe? Georgie? U'i? Mirry?" Her eyes go back and forth to everyone. "Gabriel." She snaps around and stares at me. "What was he doing to you? What did they do?"

I look at the floor. "Nothing." I say.

"You sure?" She says, forcing her voice to be soft and kind. "You can tell me you know."

I'm not a rat. "Yeah. I'm good." I stand up and walk away.

"You're not going to eat?" Grandma asks me as I open the same door I fell into. I shake my head at her and leave the kitchen.

I don't want to be in here anymore.

SEVEN

I'm outside throwing rocks at an old tree when they find me. The cousins. The little ones who were in line in front of me. "Whatcha doing out here?" A little boy who looks like he's about five asks.

"Nothing." I say. Boom goes another rock right up to the branches.

"Looks like you're throwing rocks to me." He says.

"Man you're a genius you know that?" I say. *You're mean, Gabriel.* Throw another rock.

"Grandma and Grandpa won't like that you're out here throwing rocks." The boy says.

I throw another one.

The boy scrunches his face and looks up into the branches. "You're going to get in trouble. Grandpa says that— there's an 'io nest up in that tree."

"What's that?" I ask. *I have no idea what that is.*

"It's a hawk?" The boy's answer makes me believe he's not even sure of what an 'io is himself.

"So?" I throw another rock up into the branches. *Hawaii doesn't have hawks. Do they?*

"Grandma says the 'io is our aumakua." He pronounces the word ow-mah-koo-ah. "That means it's sacred for our— for our family."

"It means it's a guardian. It watches us." A girl's voice says from behind me.

I don't turn around because I know from the tone that she's one of them. She's that one who told me to go in, the one with the goofy sounding name, the girl they call U'i.

"That's pretty creepy, don't you think? A sacred guardian bird who watches you?" I say and grab a rock the size of my fist. I toss it in the air a few times to feel its heft *it's way heavier than the other ones* and hurl it up into the tree. This one does something, breaks something. A branch cracks, snaps, and then something falls down. It looks like a big pile of dead twigs.

"No!" The girl screams and pushes me out of her way. It *is* U'i. I knew it. Because of her shove I fall (again) but does she care? No. "Oh my God, oh my God!" She's yelling, as if she is being murdered. She turns around and stares at me. Tears are pouring out of her reddened eyes. "There are two babies in here Gabriel, *two of them!*"

I walk closer and see what I already knew. Two really ugly and kind of big babies. *What did I do?* "I-I-how was I supposed to know?"

"*They* told you to watch out!" U'i screeches. Her fingers

72

are raised, nails sharp as talons. I wonder if she's taking on the shape of this aumakua thing.

"Wait-wait-wait-wait-wait. What is this? What is happening?" A woman's voice is yelling from right behind me. I turn around. *Everyone* is outside. The woman's voice belongs to Grandma. "Auwe. Auwe!" She looks at all of us kids. "Whose fault is this? Whose doing?"

All fingers point at me. "He was throwing rocks at it." The little boy rats me out.

"Auwe, Gabriel. Auwe." Now she's crying. "Do you know the gravity of what you've just done?"

I shake my head.

Grandma is wringing her hands. "You brought down the house of our aumakua. Our protectors. The 'io is precious to our 'ohana because when we are lost, they help to guide us back to the right path. It's been that way for us for centuries. And these birds, they've been coming back to us in this house for as long as I can remember. They don't bother anyone. They stay right up there in the nest of their kupuna. Their elders. The very same nest. *They* are the reason we built our house this way. In the shape of a circle. Using the bones of the original house. It's symbolic. We wanted to provide the framework so all of you can live and thrive. But now, after all these years, you've scared them away. Their makua, their parents will never come back."

Great. As if I didn't feel bad enough.

I want to run. Run somewhere far where I won't have any worries where I don't do everything wrong where no one will bother me. I want to go find Makena. Wherever she is. But I don't. *I'm a wuss, remember?* "Sorry." I mumble. I mean it even though the words don't come out like I want them to. I clear my throat and try again. "I'm sorry." Still sounds unconvincing. The baby birds are crying now. *At least they're alive.* My eyes look at Grandpa. My Uncles. My Dad. Mom. *I'm dead.* "You want me to put it back in the tree?"

"Birds don't touch their babies once a human's scent is on them. Genius." The little boy tells me.

"What can I do?" I ask my Grandma. "I want to help."

"Just go away." The little kid says. "Go away and don't never-ever come back!"

So I run. And this time my feet move. Grandpa rushes, catches me, holds on. "It's okay. It's okay, boy. You okay. You good." I melt into his hot arms. I feel safe. Grandpa holds my shoulders, smiles into my eyes. "You like see your new home?"

I don't have a home anymore. I shake my head no.

"You no like see yo' new ha-le?"

"No." I tell him. I want to go back to my old ha-le. The one we left behind. I want my old friends. I want to see Deanna again. I want— I want Makena to suffer along with me.

"Well then," Grandpa whispers, "let's jus' take a walk. Cool down." He looks at the others, waves his right arm in the air and walks next to me. He's quiet for a while, as if he's thinking of the right words to say. When he opens his mouth, he asks simply, "why you so hu-hu?" I have no idea what he said and the expression on my face must have given it away because he's laughing. "Hu, yo' moddah nevah teach you guys notting I guess. Huhu means mad. Upset."

Oh. I get it. But I don't want to talk about it. "I didn't do that thing—back there—I didn't do it on purpose." My voice

74

sounds foreign and thin in the Hawaiian air; weird because it sounded perfectly normal back home.

"You still worried about dat?" He asks. "Ah. We worry about all dat latahs. Anyt'ing can be fix you know." I follow along behind him, back down the side of his massive house.

I walk one foot in front of the other when we come to the path that looks like islands floating in a sea of lava, and even though I really want to hop across them, even though I want to feel the long stretch of my legs spreading over the large flat stones, I trudge like a grown up through the grass, the path, through everything without giving a care about using any type of imagination. *Don't want him to think I need to grow up.*

We get to the back fence, which is tall and made out of shiny white vinyl. Grandpa undoes the latch and it swings open into a huge grassy lawn. He closes it and I am surprised to see several different houses in the backyard. Grandpa calls two of them, 'cottages' but they're more like two story townhouses attached to the big house's long balcony by trellises.

It reminds me a little of a hotel we stayed in when we went to Florida once. The place with the bedbug infestation. I laughed and laughed when Makena got bit but cried when it happened to me. Those things suck in more ways than one.

In the center of this cluster of homes is a big green yard and a funky shaped swimming pool with black rocks, slides, and waterfalls. Some younger kids are playing in it but none take notice of us as we walk by them. *I'll bet the water is warmer than it should be.*

We continue walking towards the end of the yard until we get to the part where it starts dipping down a bit. There are other structures that are separate from the rest and are on the lower part of a hillside. One of these is a potting shed filled with seeds and junk. Attached to this shed is a greenhouse filled with shelves and tables covered with plants and flowers. A little further below this is the guesthouse. Grandpa calls it that, but in actuality, it's bigger than our old house back in Cali, and about as long as the main house at the top of the driveway. It's single story and pretty much takes up the bottom of the hill.

"Every room in dis house get one view of da ocean." Grandpa says, slipping his feet out of his flip-flops. "We usually keep all da doors open 'cuz we all 'ohana but if you like lock 'em, can." He reaches out to open the double doors. "Dis was supposed to be Nalu's house but since your Daddy stay in one wheelchair we moved him out an' put him in one of da two stories." *No wonder Mom's brother is so angry.* "Little bit old but nice. Get everything you need- three bedrooms, two bathrooms, living room, kitchen, closets, shed, and one carport on da side."

I know better now so I kick my shoes off and leave them out on the front porch. Papa is already inside walking around. I won't admit it out loud but I do feel pretty excited to see where we're going to live. I mean, my heart isn't fluttering or anything like that, but for the first time since we got here, I can't wait to see something.

I step up into the house and look around. It's neater than I thought it would be. I mean, maybe it's not as nice as the Grandparent's house, but it's enough to make me smile a little. The floors are mostly carpet, except for the entryway, which is covered with light colored bamboo. And it's nice carpet, thick and shaggy in different colors of brown and gray—the kind that you just want to throw yourself down and roll around on. *Don't know how Dad's going to get around in it but it's okay if he can't because it means more space for me.*

The old man pulls on the strings at the end of the living room drapes and treats me to a broad view of both the mountain and the ocean. The room is positioned in such a way that the view can be seen from three places: the living room, the dining room, and the kitchen. There's a balcony, which Grandpa stepped out on with enough room to fit a jumbo-sized barbecue grill and a whole bunch of edible plants. I only know this because that's what is out there. A jetted spa in the left hand corner next to a tall railing is just the filling in the flaky pastry we had earlier.

I'm ashamed to admit it, but after seeing that, I run from room to room like a yappy little dog. My parent's room has a huge walk-in closet that I know Mom will love, and a good-sized bathroom with two sinks, a huge shower and a soaking tub big enough for an elephant. But even better than that, is it's far away from my room, which also has it's own bathroom.

My room is probably the size of the living room, and it has tall sliding windows that go from my shins to a foot away from the ceiling. I look outside and see the boats and the birds in the trees. *Ugh. I'm so dumb.* My thoughts go back to the two ugly baby birds on the driveway and suddenly, seeing my new house isn't so fun anymore. I walk to the spare room. The room I unintentionally call for Makena to come and look at.

"Makena, check out your room!" I say. *So stupid. Calling her like she's here.* I hear the patio door close.

"What you said, boy? You okay?" Grandpa's asking.

"I'm fine." I mutter. *I'm such an idiot.*

"Guess you found yo' room?" He's banging around in the kitchen now.

"Yeah." I call. I'm still in Makena's room. It's sort of in the middle of the house, at the front of the hallway. It has the same kind of big squarish closet that she had back home and a bathroom with a claw foot bathtub. Her bedroom also has a sliding door that leads to it's own patio area. I roll it open, take in the air.

"Hello?" A voice says from the front door.

"Who dat?" Grandpa asks, but I don't have to ask. I know Mom's voice when I hear it.

"Mom said to tell you that the baby birds are doing fine. Says she wants to take care of them until they get better."

I wait for Grandpa to say something back to Mom but he doesn't.

Mom's footsteps are prancing around the house. "Daddy I'm talking to you. Why aren't you answering me?"

Grandpa is quiet for a while and then he mutters, "Who cares about the birds?"

"Daddy!" Mom sounds upset.

"Main thing is that the boy is alright." Grandpa growls.

"The boy—*that boy* almost killed the birds." Mom snaps.

"*That boy* is a good boy. He's a good boy, Haunani."

"You don't even *know* him." Mom cries out in a way I never heard her bawl.

"Enough!" He says. He closes his eyes, and I imagine he's counting to ten just like Mom used to do before we lost Makena. When he opens them, it's as if a different man speaks. "Well, dis is da best that we could do for you folks and main t'ing is dat it's

78

yours, Haunani. Nobody can take it away. You no need worry about dat." His footsteps are moving to the front door. "And one day it will belong to *that boy*. *His* name is on da estate plan fo' dis house. Remembah dat." *Why me? Why not Mom?* The front door croaks my name. *Gaaaaabe*. "Mama and I went shopping foah some extra stuff befoah you came, so you get all kinds of new stuff like one washing machine, one dryah, one icebox and one fancy stove. Oh an get planny food in da cupboards an' some in da fridge. We bought you folks dat as one housewarming. Oddah den dat girl, it's up to you. Keep da house nice, I no like see one wreck."

I peek around the corner and see him brushing her hair back with his right hand, and spy Dad in the hallway with his head staring upward at Grandpa. "Haunani. I'm happy you and your 'ohana are finally home. Just, don't… just let da boy be. Okay?" He squeezes his eyes tightly and pinches the bridge of his nose that are near the corners of his eyes. "I wish you folks happiness, love and one good future. Well," he claps his hands together and the sound he makes echoes through the house. "See you den." I watch as he slips out into the early evening breeze and shuts the door softly behind him.

Mom sees me watching from Makena's doorway and sneers.

EIGHT

It's official. I thoroughly hate it here.

No one told me we wouldn't have Internet in this house. No Wi-Fi, no television, no video games, no movies, no one to talk to, nothing. Just a whole bunch of old Hawaiian history books, and a stupid, boring journal written by Makena (when she was nine-years-old) that I've already read cover to cover. Twice. I'm surprised we even have electricity. And since we sold *all* of our stuff prior to moving here, I have nothing to do but look out of windows at the sky and the air. I would tell everyone back home that I am currently living in a luddite compound, but I have no way to tell them about how it is to live with these techphobic freaks because we have no phone and my parents won't let me use theirs.

So for the past seven days, I've been babysitting my parents. That might be pretty rude sounding but it's how I'd describe our new routine. First, I wake up, make breakfast—not just for me, but for them, and then I serve them. Sure, it's only cereal most of the time, but it's almost all I know how to cook.

I eat all by myself in the kitchen, go back and get their dishes, scrape them, load the dishwasher, and steal the job section from the paper at the gate and stick it in the bathroom so they can catch the hint and comb through it. I just want them out of my hair, you know?

Every now and then I'll run into one of Mom's family members when I'm staring at the sky outside or wading around in the pool by myself, but I still don't know anyone's names, and I run away right when I see them because I'm afraid they'll ask me how come they never see Mom. I don't want to be the one to tell them that she hasn't left the bed since we got here. How I think it's sad because she smothers that jar-o–Makena so much that she never has time for anyone or anything anymore. No time for the outdoors, no time to socialize, no time to eat. I don't want to say how bored I am of her, and how I sometimes want to take Makena's cremains and throw a touchdown with it just so she will pay attention to me. How I single handedly unpacked our house, how I feed the three of us, (again, so what if it's cereal?) How much I actually miss having my sister—my actual flesh and blood sister— around because God damn it I am alone. *And I don't care if that offends you, Mom. Dad.*

Everyone else is in summer school, but I'm not enrolled because my parents probably know that I'm too smart to bother with all of that, so I am forced to either sit by myself in my bedroom, to sit outside and pick plugs of grass from their beds or worse— to read one of those books in the living room cabinet.

But at least Grandma's not mad at me anymore. Not since Uncle Nalu got the big birds to come back. Supposedly, Mom's brother climbed up the tree and put the babies and the nest back on the same branch they were on. Grandma said he went way up to the top, and that at one point she was afraid he was going to die because he was wearing gloves—probably because he was scared of spreading his fungus to the little ones—and she said that wearing gloves pretty much means there is zero traction, but he made it and the mother and father 'io, according to her, are back to guard the house. She named the two parents Hina and Lono and the little cousins call the babies Peep and Peeper because they're 'creative' like that.

Right now, I'm trying not to think of them though. I'm trying to figure out how to get messages to my friends. Specifically Deanna. I don't have any paper and I know my parents don't either but since I'm the one who went and unpacked everything I go to Makena's room because I *know* she has paper. Makena was a paper collector and since Mom and Dad wanted to keep all of her junk, we boxed it up and brought it with us. Even though more than ninety percent of my stuff was tossed out or donated, we still had her stuff like her paper—lined, dotted, graph, blank, in all different colors with all kinds of characters ranging from uncomfortably surly, to plain innocent, to annoyingly happy. And her pen collection was even worse. How a person could need so many pens with so many different shades of ink is creepy to me. Real creepy. And indecisive.

I wonder if it's okay that I go through her stuff. I know if she were here she'd be mad at me unless she was there with me. And I believe that she might even haunt me if I went through with it, but I'll go through with it anyway. I am so desperate right now that I sneak into Mom and Dad's room. They're both asleep. As usual. I see Makena's jar right between Mom and Dad on their bed. The whole room reeks of cheese, armpits, and urine. I try not to puke as I lean over Dad *don't make a sound, don't make a sound, grab it ohhhh grab it before it rolls and they wake up, safe*. It's in my arms. I fan the potency back towards them and seal them back in their darkened crypt.

This is the first time I've actually held this jar-o-Makena but like I said, I'm desperate. I put her down on the table near her bed. *There. Now you can't say you weren't here when I went through your stuff.* I sift. I scamper. I click and scribble with the pens until I find the hue I want and then I sprawl out on her bed and compose a letter using paper adorned with a pretty rainbow to my sweetie. I chose a red pen with kisses all over it.

> Dear Deanna,
>   I am in hell. My parents don't want me, everybody hates me and all I do is sit around all day and wait til night comes to take me away. I feel like a slave because I'm the only one around here who does anything and I'm writing to you like a dork only because I can't get in contact with you any other way. We are disconnected from the entire planet and even when I sneak my parent's cell phones, they won't work because there is no reception here.

I reread what I wrote. *Too negative.* I crumple it up. Start again. Green paper, angry ninja with a sword right at the center of the lines, licorice scented pen.

Dear Deanna,
I wish I was home with you. I really really miss you. If and when I see you again, I plan to hold you for a long, long time.

    Nope. Too feminine. Girls don't dig that kind of stuff. Crumple it up. Again.

    Puke pink paper, desperate for attention dog, red stripes, purple, bruised face colored pen.

Dear Deanna,
Makena being dead really stinks.

Arrrgh. Diarrhea. I grab another paper; a plain white traditional piece of folder paper with the pink stripe on the left side to indicate that the margin starts there and the thin blue stripe on the right side to tell you to end your words there. That beautiful piece of paper with the three holes that done correctly will last inside your three ring binder for ages, but insert it incorrectly and it will cut itself loose from your inept fingers and find its way to the floor. Regular blue ball point generico in my left hand. With my best and slowest print, I scratch:

Dear Deanna,
    Hi. I know I've been quiet since I moved but I've been really busy. Hawaii is great. It's beautiful here, lots of fun beaches and stuff to do. People here are so awesome. I love them. My whole entire

family especially. Every day is like a sunny vacation. Remember when you said that things were going to be different when I left? I'm writing this letter to show you that you are right. I think mailing letters like this is more fun, and different so let's 'talk' like this from now on, okay? I will send you pictures of myself doing totally awesome stuff soon okay?

I hope you're not missing me too much.

Aloha,

Your Gabe.

Yes. I read it again. *Yes, yes.* And again. *Yes, yes, yes.* It's a success. I address it, stamp it with one of those cartoon stamps in my sister's pencil case, and put Makena's stuff away. I slip the letter into my pocket and say, "Thank you Makena," to the jar, trying my best to speak nice and civil to her for once. Trying to make my words count. "Oh, by the way. This is your new room. Do you like it? It's got its own patio and one of those old style bathtubs you said you wanted. I could've taken this room easily but I knew it was meant for you."

I put her jar right on the center of her bed and smooth the wrinkles out of the sheets. It grosses me out to look at her cremains. All that dust, all that ground up skin and powder. So I run into the living room and grab an album filled with pictures of Makena. Pictures are basically the only tangible things besides all of her material possessions that we have left.

I find a photo that we have doubles of, a smiling one of
her. Just her. It's a close-up of her face—so close I can see her
freckles and her moles. It was taken by her friend who used it to
make her the fake I.D. that Mom and Dad knew about but never
punished her for because she always got away with everything. I
close the album, put it away and trek back into the room quietly.

If Mom and Dad aren't going to buy Makena a proper
urn, then I am going to try and make this one look pretty. Hey,
I said *try*. I found some rubber cement earlier when I was
looking through Makena's things so I know where to go. My
left hand goes into the big zippered pouch, comes out with an
amber colored generic branded bottle. I unscrew the cap as fast
as I can. If I'm going to be all top secret about this I have to be
incognito. I carefully crack one side open and make sure that the
brush is attached to the cover because more than often, with this
brand, it's not. The brush is there, *thank God* but the smell—the
toxic, fuel charged, chemical warning of disastrous danger is
threatening to end this mission. I turn the picture over, brush
a thick layer of glue on it *gah it's clumping* and try my best to
spread it out evenly. The hair from the brush is getting on the
picture but I'm in a rush so I leave it alone, turn it over, and slap
that puppy onto the bottle. There. Much better. At least people
will know what it really is.

Or will they?

I dump out her pens and find one that says, 'permanent.'
Like her regular writing instruments, she has so many of these
to choose from that I just grab a whole bunch and write with my
best tagging hand above her picture: Makena Nalani Foster. I
admire my work. It came out pretty nice. But I can't help feeling

that the other side is too naked. I stand it up and draw a picture of a rainbow, an ocean, and a dolphin on the blank section. *Much better*. Underneath, I write the words:

Died too young

My head is spinning now so I open the patio door and let the room breathe while I put Makena's stuff away again. "Either Mom and Dad are going to hate it, or they'll love it." I say to Makena's photo. "Which one do you think it'll be?"

As I'm climbing to put the glue back on the bookshelf where I found it, I pull on a shoebox and it pours scraps of paper out all over my head. *Ugh. I hope that noise doesn't wake Mom and Dad.* I stand still and wait. Nothing. I shove the papers back into the shoebox and glance at a few of them: song lyrics, poems, sketches, and a couple of letters. *Juicy.* I push them back in the box and pop the lid back on.

A crash in the other room doesn't even give me time to think. The box gets kicked under the bed for later, and the mess I made is clumsily tossed on a random shelf on the bookcase. A thump, some heavy heel pounding, and another loud thud follow this sound. My head is spinning around and around, my eyes are darting around the room the way a lizard's does when it hears a fly, and my feet are planted straight on the ground. I'm getting ready to sneak out of there when I hear my mom bawling. Scared, I put Makena back on the pillow and back away.

Before I can open my mouth I hear Mom opening hers. "She's gone Gavin I can't find her anywhere. Did you push her over the edge? Did you get rid of Makena?"

"Marcel, you know I would never do that." He's cooing.

"You said you never wanted her. You even asked my

parents if they wouldn't mind adopting her!" Mom's voice is quivering.

"I never meant that." Dad pleads.

"You meant it. You meant it you liar. You *liar!"* Mom's voice is so rough it sounds like it's tearing up her dried lips. "You wanted me to give her up just like I," Mom's voice is muffled, like Dad is doing something to her.

My stomach feels queasy, jolts up, ties itself in knots. "Mom." I run to their room. *Dad said he killed a bunch of people when he was away. He could be killing her for all I know.* "Mom." I tap on the door. "Are you okay?"

I don't even have to wait for her answer. "I am not okay, Gabriel. I am *not okay.* Your sister is gone. Missing. I don't know where she is. Oh, I don't know where she is." She's angry but I'm glad she's fine. I don't know how she's going to react when I give Makena back, though. But I know she'll go crazy if I don't. I scamper back to Makena's room, grab the newly decorated bottle and tap on the door again. This time, it swings right open. And there on the other side is Mom. "She's right here." I say, trying to seem calm; happy even.

Mom's jaw drops down to her chest. "What in God's name are you doing with my baby?" She's glaring at me and tugging at the bottle, trying hard to get it out of my hands. She's got a good grip of it and is pulling it so hard, it makes me hold tighter. I don't want to just let it go of it and watch my Mom fly off to outer space, (or the floor, whichever beckons her first) so I hold onto it for dear life. "Give it to me now!" She shrieks, and yanks the urn so hard that it slips through the air like a peeled potato and falls back on the bed. Mom lifts it up, inspects it. Other than my beautification project, everything looks immaculate. Mom's face turns beet red and her eyes are wider than I've seen them in a while. "I don't believe you! You hateful kid! Get out of here, do you hear me? Get out and don't come back!"

I look at Dad, whose eyes are full of heartbreak and hurt and I slip out of that house without looking at either of them. I don't know where to go so I wander around on the property for a little while, feed rocks to the pigeons, try to spot the 'io I almost killed up in the tall tree with the red flowers, and wait by the mailbox for the mailman to come so I can hand deliver the letter to Deanna that was shoved in my pants. The little mail truck grumbles down the road and the lady takes it and rolls away without a smile. I stand there on the side of the road, tasting her dust, watching until her mail truck is a speck of dust, watching cars drive up and down the road because I don't know where else to go. I kill a few ants with my fingernail while contemplating life, and after more wandering around the property; I find peace inside my Grandparent's carport.

NINE

I'm fingering the dusty tools on the shelves; counting cans of spray oil that are missing their tops and nozzles when I hear footsteps. "What's up, new boy?" Joe-Joe the bully folds his arms across his chest and shoots me a game show host's smile.

The rest of the cousins are with him, and they laugh at his comments. Everyone but U'i, anyway. "Nice to see you outside." She says. "You're pretty anti-social you know that?"

I don't feel like talking to anyone but she seems like she's trying to be nice so I tell her, "yeah. It's just hard."

Joe-Joe smacks his older brother on his shoulder. "That's 'cuz you da new boy."

"Stop calling him that." U'i narrows her eyes at him, and puffs out her lips. I wonder what makes her want to defend me. I don't know her, she doesn't know me and besides, I *am* a new boy. She turns to mc with her hands on her hips. "That don't make you mad?"

I shake my head. Shrug my shoulders. "Naw, it's chill.

Why would I be mad?" I try to play it cool and act like I'm happy that they gave me a new nickname.

"Because niu in Hawaiian means coconut." *And, so?* U'i's rolling her eyes at me. "Duh. Joe-Joe doesn't mean new as in brand new, he means niu as in coconut." She raises one thin eyebrow at me. "Do you like being called a coconut? Because if you do, then stop me from defending you right now."

"What's so bad about being called a coconut?" I wonder out loud.

U'i sighs like the ocean. "You for serious?"

I think it's a fruit? Or is it a vegetable? Or maybe it's a nut. If he's trying to be insulting, he's either trying to say one of three ignorant things: I'm nuts, I'm fruity, or worse—I'm a vegetarian. U'i must be reading my mind because she's standing right next to grandpa's black Porshe frowning at me. "Coconut means you're brown on the outside, white on the inside."

What does that even mean? I don't know what to say. All my life I was accepted. Almost everyone I knew treated me like a friend. And they weren't even related to me. I shake off the comment and walk away, leaving the four of them to stare after me.

"Ho, sorry ah, niu boy!" Joe-Joe is laughing like a moron and slapping his knee in delight.

"Shut up, you guys!" U'i whines.

"Fine den. How 'bout sweet bread? Sweet bread bettah fo' you?" Joe's brother George yells.

"Or malassadas." The little girl, Mirry shrieks with laughter.

"You guys so stupid." U'i snaps.

I don't care if she's trying to defend me. I don't owe her anything. I'm not trying to be anyone's friend. I'm walking down the other side of the driveway where I have never gone yet.

"Nah. Niu boy is perfect fo' one haole mainland like him." Joe-Joe says.

And then boom. It's like someone lit a match under my skin. I spin around on my heel and book it over to him with my fists clenched, and my arms ready to swing.

"Fight! Fight! Fight!" George circles his hands around his mouth but before anything happens, Mom's brother Uncle Nalu pulls himself out from whatever rock he was sitting under and throws himself in front of Joe-Joe with brute force.

"Fricka calm down." He says to the bigger cousin, and shoves him to the side with his back. To me he snarls, "brah- you bettah think twice before you pick a fight wit' Joe-Joe. He going buss you up big time. He won trophies for scrapping cuz. MMA, boxing, jiu-jitsu, you name it he does it. If he *taps* you, you guarantee bleed. An' you," He thwacks Joe-Joe across the chest hard. "Give da boy a break. He's new."

I'm not sure if he's citing fact, or if he's just trying to be 'funny' so I ask him. "What's that supposed to mean?"

Uncle Nalu narrows his eyes at me. "Eh, jus' shaddup already, ah niu boy."

꒰ ✺ ꒱

I'm halfway up the road when Uʻi catches up with me. "Hey, you. Slow down," she bosses. I ignore her. Keep on walking the same pace. "Hey buttface." She yells again. "I said slow down."

I stop. Makena used to call me buttface.

"What's up with you?" She says when she catches up to me.

I don't say anything. I feel like someone owes me an apology if I'm going to start talking.

"If you think I'm going to apologize to you, you can forget it." She says. *Whoa. Can she read my mind?* She's looking at me as if she can. "I stuck up for you back there and besides,

I never apologize for other people. It's not my fault if someone feels like being a dickopotamus."

Now I'm not saying anything because I don't know what to say. She's looking at me. She's raising her left eyebrow. Her lips are pursed. I'd better say something. "Sorry." *Wait. Why am I saying sorry? You're so dumb, Gabe. Dumb, dumb, dumb, dumb, dumb.*

"It's okay." She just takes my apology like it was hers to begin with. I hate myself for saying those words. She's smiling at me now. "So are you coming?"

"Coming to what?" There my voice goes again, escaping from that faux-friendly Mr. Bean looking face I was cursed with again. I feel my left eyebrow lifting up Leonard Nimoy style. Hers lifts as well. I feel as if the fur on our faces are having weird conversations of their own.

"Dinner." She answers, with a voice as flat as the cement pad we're standing on. "We have dinner together every Sunday. It's one of Grandpa's rules."

I nod. If it has something to do with Grandpa, I'll do it. He seems nice enough. "Sure."

She's looking at me like I'm a freak again. "So yeah. How old are you, again?"

"Thirteen and a half." I reply.

"Huh." She says, her voice dripping with sass. "I thought you were older than that." She eyes me up and down and shrugs. "Well, you're still too young for my friend so don't even think about her."

I look around U'i. Either she has one of those invisible friendships I've heard people say they had in preschool, or she's hiding someone in her slightly bushy brown hair. "I hate to tell you this but… I don't see anyone." I finally say.

She gives me the stink eye, and her top lip curls up. It makes her pretty face look really ugly. "Duh. She's not coming 'til dinner."

"What time is it?" I ask dully.

"I don't know, do I look like I'm wearing a watch?" She snaps.

I stare at her wrists for what— I don't know. "No, I mean. I mean what time is the dinner?"

"Oh," she says as if I'm now a bother. "It's at five."

I look at her the way she looks at me. "I guess we'd better go back home."

She shrugs, pulls her phone out of her pocket and looks at it. "Yeah we should. It's about half past three." I'm irritated, but wondering if Uʻi's phone has reception. Ever since Mom confiscated my cell phone back in Cali, I've been lost.

My feet follow her as we head back up the road to our grandparent's house. My mouth opens, but her voice comes out instead. "You better change soon." *Why? I have clothes on.* "And you better bring something." *Like what?* "Hawaiian style," she explains, "you always bring something to eat with you when you go to somebody's house." There she goes with the mind reading again. "You *do* have something to eat, don't you? *Please* tell me you have food." I don't know what we have. I do a mental search of our pantry in my head but all I can see is my Mom and Dad crying over a painted jar full of Makena.

"Actually," I say, breaking my silence. "I don't know what we have."

"So go look."

Yeah let me just go look at the floor while I get a good old fashioned yelling at. "I don't know if I can come home yet." *There. I said it.*

"For real?" She smiles. "You serious?" My nod makes her laugh. "What did you do, open the windows to let in the sun or something?"

"No, actually," I start to laugh too. She moves forward, waiting to hear what I did. "I drew this thing all over Makena…" I say, with a hearty smile on my face.

She looks cross with me. "What do you mean by, you drew a thing. All over. Makena?"

"I mean I took some permanent markers and drew pictures and added a picture on top of Makena's ash thing."

"You mean an urn." U'i corrects, and looks at me like she's waiting for me to say it with her. "It's called an urn. Not an ash thing."

"Whatever." I say. She has no clue. An urn is something sacred and special. The thing Makena is in is just an airtight mayo container with a plastic screw top lid.

"How old are you?" She asks again. I don't tell her because dang it I already told her two minutes ago. She frowns. "You need to go back to Kindergarten or something. Come with me. We'll go bake a patty cake or something."

We walk past another carport, but this one is absent of cars and tools. This particular carport is filled with canoes and surfboards. U'i must see me looking because she asks, "you're from Cali, right?"

"Right."

"You must know how to surf and sponge then, yeah?"

I nod. *What am I doing? I have no idea how to surf and I have no idea what sponge even means.*

"Cool. Maybe we can go down after summer school tomorrow before we paddle."

Paddle? I have no idea what she's talking about. If it were Makena talking, I would straight up ask her, 'what choo talking about, woman?' but it's my cousin so I say, "sure, that sounds nice."

"Wait. Did your parents put you in summer school?" She asks. Man she's nosy. Every five seconds there's a question mark flying out of her face. I shake my head and she goes wild. "Wait. You've been here a week already. What have you been doing?"

I pause. I did a lot of thinking. A lot of picking up broken pieces. A lot of walking on eggshells. A lot of trying to keep my parents happy. A lot of unpacking and a lot of putting things away. "Nothing." I answer.

"Wow. You would think your parents would be on you about going to summer school."

Who are you, the principal? "Naw. They're more concerned about Makena right now."

Now she's staring at me with pity eyes. I hate pity eyes. "Makena's dead." She says.

Really? As if I didn't know that! "Well, she's… you know… they're just going through some things right now."

"And what about you?" She asks.

Leave me alone!

"How are *you* doing?" Uʻi is trying to get too close to me. I don't answer and it's all Makena's fault. She was the one who said I was selfish, that I never thought about anyone else but myself. I didn't want to move here, I was so against it. I fought so hard with her and I killed her—I was so selfish. Me. No, I'm done with thinking about myself. With talking about myself. What does it matter how I'm doing? How *I'm* dealing with things? We're two feet away from U'i's front door now but I already know that I'm not going in.

"You know what, make the stupid patty cake yourself." I'm not shocked one bit that any of those words are coming out of my mouth. Makena always said I had a bad attitude. I guess she was right. Again. "Later," I say with ice in my throat.

"But what about your parents?" My cousin's asking. "Won't they get mad that you're back home again?" *Great. I told her too much.* Her face looks like she's genuinely concerned but I don't know if I can trust her. She'll probably go blabbing our conversation to everyone else and… I really don't want to think about what will happen next. Don't want to talk about it either. So this time, instead of explaining myself, I turn and run back down the trail that we just walked up on.

I bring beans. Four cans to be exact. It was pretty much all we had left in the pantry and no one in our house eats beans anyway so I figure, why not? U'i said that I had to show up with something to eat and beans is something people eat. Just not us.

When I open the door to my grandparent's house, the warm scent of turkey, onions, garlic, and sautéed mushrooms greet me. It's a little weird to me, considering it's not even

Thanksgiving yet, but I leave my shoes outside, and enter noticing that there are people already in the living room, the sitting room, and the dining area. Besides my cousins from hell, I'm still not sure what their names are, everyone else is walking around snacking on random things. No one says anything to me, but I can feel their eyes puncturing my shell, and I refuse to appear wounded.

I walk to the kitchen with my head up, put the cans of beans on the counter and stare at the labels. Lentils in water, kidney beans in water, black beans in water, white beans in water. What a nice variety. But wait—am I supposed to give them to someone? Maybe I should have asked one of the many eyes that were intent on prodding my soul out of my body.

Thinking fast, I open and close the drawers making sure not to slam them as I look for the can opener. *Don't want to draw any more attention to myself than I already am.* I finally find one on the counter, and I use it to open up each can. *Am I supposed to cook these?* I read the one closest to me. *No cooking necessary. Good.* All four are open; all lids are thrown away. *Should I pick off the labels?* I decide I should. I carefully peel them off, so that shiny silver cans is what people will see versus the ugly paper. There. Now that they're open people can tell what is what. I open a drawer, dig out a spoon, plunk it into the red beans. I grab another and another and another and plop them into each can. Stir, stir, stir until each bean makes itself known. There. Perfect. *Gabe, you are a genius.*

"What dat? Beans?" I spin around and see Grandpa smiling at me. In his face, I can see him asking me why on Earth would you bring that, and who do expect to eat it? But instead

99

he says, "okay." And helps me arrange the four cans on a crystal serving tray.

I go out to the dining table with him and he sets it down next to a white ceramic baking pan filled with steak. Grandma gives him a sharp look that softens when he looks over at me. She motions for me to stand between them, which I do, then takes my hand. My eyes close instinctively. I bow my head and listen. "E pule kākou" she says and starts to pray. This time, I know better. I don't snicker at her words even though I want to because I know there will be hell to pay if I do. "Amene. Amama ua noa," Grandma squeezes my hand and lets go. I look up and see my parents at the far end of the table. Both are wearing tight frowns on their sad, pale faces.

"Let's eat!" Uncle Nalu bellows and corrals the smaller kids towards the stack of plates. I watch him hand them out to each one; watch them make a mess out of everything. I don't bother to help, I'm too hungry for that. I grab a plate of my own and scoop the foods that I know the names of onto it. Turkey, bread *it may be purple but it's bread*, mashed potatoes, gravy.

"No beans?" Grandpa whispers.

"Brah. Who brought dis?" A woman I've never met yells, pointing to the cans in the center of the table.

I did. I want to tell her, but I look away. Doesn't matter whether or not I say anything because Grandpa gives me away by pointing at me. Everybody laughs. Suddenly, I'm not so hungry anymore. I put my plate down and take a step backward.

"You take it you eat it." The same woman squawks.

A woman who looks like she could be Mom's twin says. "No be scared of diva ovah hea," she laughs, pointing to the

lady who was asking about the beans. "Dass just Aunty Vai, yo'
Mama's big sister." She stops and looks over at my parents. "You
guys get planny history, yeah, Marcel? Yeah Gavin?" They nod
and acknowledge each other but I can sense some awkwardness
between them. "And I'm your Mommy's little sister, Aunty Jo."
She reaches out for a hug. I give her the fastest one I can and pull
back before her embrace gets tighter. I can't stop staring at her
face—she has the same oval face, the same rounded nose, the
same full lips, only, *her* eyes sparkle. "Is my Uʻi being nice to
you?" She asks. *She's Uʻi's mom.* I nod. "Good." She nibbles on
a piece of celery and smiles. "She's the same age as your sister
was. Just a few months apart."

I nod like I'm interested, look at my plate, pick it up off
of the table, and slink off into the kitchen. The food smelled too
inviting for me to leave it sitting anyway.

Uʻi follows me in. "I seen you bring the beans."
"Yeah. So?" I rip a piece of meat off with my fangs and

101

chew.

"How come you don't have any beans on your plate?" *She's so nosy.*

I shrug. "I don't like beans."

"So if you don't like beans, how come you're feeding them to us?"

Enough with the beans! I swallow the softened meat and try piercing her with my gaze. Nothing happens. "I don't know." I say and stick another hunk of turkey in my mouth.

She's smiling again. I hate when she smiles. "Here's my friend Napua." She says. *God she's so inappropriate. Kind of like Makena.*

I shrug again. "I already got a girlfriend." *No one in the world could be prettier than Deanna.*

"What was that?" U'i asks.

I look up with the intent to say something offensive but my tongue is frozen. *Napua is a lot prettier than Deanna. And by a lot I mean a lot, lot, lot.* "Hi." I croak.

She smiles. Her teeth are perfect. Two straight white rows of shiny, rectangular pearls gleaming beneath a cute nose that is hovering beneath two big almond shaped eyes with long, frilly eyelashes. Her oval face is framed by high cheekbones and topped off with a pair of perfectly shaped eyebrows and her bronze skin and long black hair brings the whole package together. *So this is what exotic looks like.* I feel like I am looking at the 'after Photoshop' image on a magazine cover. "Hi." She replies. "Napua Harper. You go to our school?"

I shake my head. *Where did I hear that last name before?* "I just moved." *Holy poly my heart is thumping. My palms are getting sweaty. I was never like this with Deanna. It's just a girl, what the heck is wrong with me?*

"Oh." She says and flicks her honey streaked hair into the air like the whole world is some kind of a commercial. "Too bad."

I want to say more to her but I don't. I want her to say more to me but she doesn't either. After a few eons of awkward silence she roams off leaving U'i in my sights again. "Yeah. So anyway, that's my friend."

"Cool." I respond, and try to go back to focusing on my plate. *Why won't my hands stop shaking? Calm down, son.*

U'i's staring at me. "Do you wanna…"

"Nope." I answer. *I don't want to cheat on Deanna. I don't want to cheat on Deanna.*

"You know, hanging out with another girl isn't cheating." U'i purrs.

How does she always know what I'm thinking? Get out of my mind you creeper! "I know." I answer coldly.

"Okay, your loss." U'i flicks her hair back in a non-commercial kind of way and raises her creeperton eyebrows up at me. "A lot of guys want her, you know."

Want her for what? She's not property. "So?" I reply. But what I really want to say is yes, I want to hang out yes I want to be around her yes I want to sit with the two of you and stare at her beautiful face all night long.

U'i shrugs and shakes her head. "Whatevs, just thought I'd let you know."

She leaves me in absolute silence. I'm half done with a purple colored dinner roll when I hear a woman in the other room saying my name. "So why don't you stick the boy in summer school, then? I mean if Gabriel is giving you that much stress, why not put him in the same school with the rest of his cousins? He should be learning, he's almost an adult, for chrissakes."

"I don't know. They might not let him in and Gavin doesn't really want him around the local kids." Mom's voice is forcing itself through the walls, as usual.

"Are you serious?" The woman snaps.

"No, no, I'm fine with it. We just thought he'd want to you know, just hang out and relax for a while. I mean summer is what kids look forward to all year right? Marcel." Dad whines. "Marcel. Can we talk? Privately?"

Mom doesn't say anything. No one does. I strain my ears waiting for a sound but I don't hear a word. Finally, Grandpa's voice cracks the ice. "We have paddling tomorrow for all the kids. Season started already but we can still throw him in one race. Would be nice if da boy can come spend time wit' his cousins. Get to know everyone. Get to know his sport, his culture. No need take him summer school if you no like, relax is good too but at least let me take him paddling."

I can taste the discomfort in the air. Mom's going to say no. I can feel it.

Dad beats her to it. "Yeah. I mean, yes Mr. Kane, sir, Gabe will do it."

A cheer rises in the air, and it shocks my skin so much, it turns to goose flesh. "Mai-ka-i no. Superb."

"And Jo—maybe," Dad continues, "maybe you can find out if we can still enroll him in that summer school?"

"Shoots!" Comes the reply.

I swallow the last of my purple bread. I don't think I like this.

TEN

Aunty Jo had her crazy daughter bang at our door at five thirty in the morning. Mom must've gotten up and let her in because the next thing I know, Uʻi was in my bedroom jumping up and down on my bed. "Stop, Makena." I groaned, and she did.

"You just called me Makena." She said.

I buried my head under my pillow. *So what? You try to act just like her, might as well call you by her name.* The covers start coming off and the cold air races across my skin. "Stop." I growl.

"Wake up or I'm going to fart on your bed." She says.

Who does that? "Whatever." I say from beneath the softness of the pillow. At least I can't smell anything through the cotton filter sitting on my face. Wait… "what the actual hell Uʻi? That's so sick!" I'm up and she's laughing at me. She probably thinks I'm fanning it away but really I'm trying to peel the scent off of me. *Skunk scent is removed by tomato sauce right? Do we have any tomato sauce in the house?*

"Get dressed. We're going to school."

"No I'm not."

"Yes, you are. Your Mom told my Mom to take you." Uʻi

is way too cheerful.

Suddenly, the smell disappears and fear punches me in the back. I must have gotten used to the eau de Uʻi which is gross because that means its straight up living in my nostrils which also means I'll be wearing it to school. "I need to take a shower."

"So take one." She says, and continues to stand there.

"So get out." I growl but the sound that seeps out from between my teeth sounds more like a invitation to keep acting dumb.

"Fine." She says and leaves my room. "But hurry up or my Mom will be really pee'd. She's on her rags you know."

What the heck are rags? Never mind. I don't want to know. "Whatever. Just go." I close my door and start throwing things around. Is Napua going to be there? Duh of course she is. She's the one who asked me if I was going to school. I grab whatever isn't too wrinkled and run to the bathroom. *Quick shower, quick dry, quick everything before that dumb nosy girl comes running in here again.* Clothes are on and I'm out my bedroom door. And then it dawns on me that I don't have a bag, or books, or pens. Everything I had I gave to Deanna so she could remember me better. *Wish she gave me something to remember her.* I walk to my sister's bedroom and find Uʻi going through the bags in my sister's closet. "What are you doing?"

She jumps. I guess she isn't psychic like I thought she was. "I-I was just looking."

"Through my sister's stuff?" I ask. "Why?"

Uʻi shrugs. "I don't know. I just wanted to see what she was like."

"Why not ask me instead of looking through her things?"

I yank the bag she's holding away from her and she flies forward. I don't care. I wasn't there to defend my sister while she was living, but I'm sure going to defend her now. "This stuff doesn't belong to you. It's private property. Private means not for you."

"I know." She whines.

"This belongs to my sister." I hold the bag out in front of her and wait for her to remind me again that Makena is dead and that she can't possibly have anything anymore. She doesn't.

"I am your sister." She yells and then claps her hands over her mouth.

"You will never be my sister." *Wait did she say she's my sister, or she's like my sister?* "You'll never be *like* my sister," I correct myself. "So stop trying to take her place!"

U'i doesn't say anything, just takes off running. I don't follow her because something about her just isn't right. When I emerge from Makena's room both of my parents are out of bed looking at me.

"Gabe, we need to talk." Mom's saying.

"Not now." I say, and walk to the front door.

Dad removes his face from his palm and says, "Gabriel. There's something you need to know."

"What?" I ask. He's not saying anything and she isn't either. It's too early to play these kinds of games and then I notice they're both falling apart in their own ways. Mom is scratching her arms and Dad is shrinking in his wheelchair and wringing his hands. Watching them makes me nervous, makes me want to run somewhere far away.

I'm tired of being the glue. I'm tired of watching you like this. You're supposed to be the parents you're supposed to take

108

care of me. The air is stale I need to get out I can't breathe I can't breathe I don't care what they say I don't need to know I don't need to know.

"I don't want to know anything!" I yell and turn the doorknob to the left. "Just leave me alone!" I'm out in the driveway waiting for the lady with the hand basket to deliver me to hell.

ELEVEN

Dear Deanna,

Went to summer school today. It's a middle school combined with a high school so we have all kinds of little kids walking around campus. There are security guards everywhere to break up fights and they keep us caged up like animals with all their fences around the perimeter of the school. Other than that things are awesome here. Teachers are nice. Campus is nice. Made a ton of friends in school today but there is no one here like you. Hope to hear from you soon.

Love,

Your Gabe

I don't tell Deanna that most of my teachers were half asleep when I got to my classes, and those who weren't were on their phones the entire period. And I didn't say anything about the fight I got into at recess because some dude called me, 'niu boy', or that my lip was swollen and bleeding but I don't remember anything that happened because I blacked out and went all crazy arms on the guy. I didn't tell her that they suspended me for two days for fighting on the first day of summer school and how they said that when I came back I would be assigned to a counselor for grief and anger management counseling. She doesn't need to know about it. I don't want to worry her.

"It's not like him." Aunty Jo told the principal when she came to get me. *Like she would know.* On our way to her beat up Corolla, she took me by the big biceps I'm bound to have one day and shook me hard. "What is your problem?"

"Nothing." I said and let my head roll all around. *Let me get shaken Gabey syndrome. I don't care.*

"That boy said he didn't do anything to you. Why the hell did you hit him?"

I could feel the scowl growing on my face. "Because he called me niu."

"So what?"

"He called me niu." I told her. *Was she dense?* "You know, niu boy."

Aunty Jo's perfectly manicured hands dropped down to her narrow hips. "Gabriel Kane Foster. You *are* new. *You* are the new boy."

She acted like she thought she was my mother. "Not new like brand new, niu like coconut niu." I explained. *I'm not a coconut. I don't know what I am but I know I am not a coconut.*

After I explained myself, Aunty Jo laughed in my face. "Gabriel. Is this about the thing Uʻi was telling me about? About your cousins giving you nicknames?" She open fist punched me right in my soon-to-be-broad shoulder. "That's not a typical thing here. Normal people don't go around calling others, 'niu.' Just Joe-Joe and Georgie."

Nice to know I'm not the only one who thinks they're not normal. "And Mirry." I added.

"Mirry's… just Mirry. I mean she's young so she doesn't know anything."

In other words she's stupid. Got it.

Aunty Jo opened the door for me, got into her busted up driver's seat and took me home. She didn't want to worry my Mom and Dad so she told me to stay and do chores for my grandparents. I cleaned and scrubbed and vacuumed but the whole time I felt like a dummy for going cray on someone who was literally calling me, 'new'.

What was I thinking? Why did that make me so pissed? What's wrong with me?

I spent the rest of the day with my brain outside of the windows. Thanks to school, I had a taste of what life was away from the estate and I wanted more. I could see the faint blue line that separated sky from water, the clouds that raced with the wind, the whitecaps that tried to catch up with them. It made me want to escape to where life was. By lunchtime, my mind was made up. I was going to do the paddling thing with everyone else.

"Go get dressed," Magical words climb out of Grandpa's lips as soon as Aunty Jo's car edges down the driveway. "You going ride with Aunty or me an' Grandma?" I want to choose him but stop when he adds, "Joe-Joe, Georgie and Nalu going come wit' us."

"I'll ride with Aunty." I whisper through chapped lips. *I sound like the crypt keeper.* "Keep her company."

"Nice boy." Grandpa says and does that thing where he rubs my head like I'm a respectable human. "See you dea."

I nod, but hold off a little because I don't feel like getting drilled or teased by any of them; who knows what they'll have to say about me today. Count to forty-one and then I'm out the door running towards the house Grandpa says is mine.

I change as quickly as I can; pull on an old pair of drawstring swimming shorts and a shabby white t-shirt, fix my hair because I know there will be girls there, and I wander outside to wait for a ride down the hill.

I watch Grandma, Grandpa, and the goons leave, and pace the front yard for a half an hour before Dad comes out to join me. "What the heck are you doing out here?" He holds his large palm over his face to screen out the bright rays of the sun and squints hard at me. "I was waiting for you in the house."

"I was, well actually I was just waiting for," I feel so nervous. And guilty. I don't want to talk to him, even though this would be the first real conversation that we've had in weeks because talking to him meant that I would have to listen to whatever it was he and Mom were trying to tell me this morning before I left for school. And even if I've been dying for one of them to say something to me, no apology needed, I didn't want to hear any words. "I'm going to paddle." I say, finally.

"We didn't finish…" he stops. "How was summer

school?"

I shrug. "It was summer school, I guess."

"Do you like it?" He asks.

I shake my head. Stop. Think hard about what to tell him.

"Look. I already know you got suspended." He sighs. "I talked to the Principal. I knew you weren't going to get along here. The people here are not our kind of people."

What kinds of people are our people, Dad? I want to say it but I frown instead. "It was a misunderstanding." I mumble. "I thought this one kid was calling me names."

"What'd he call you?" Dad asks. "He call you haole?" The way he pronounces it: how-lee; makes it sound like the name of a puppet or a cartoon character versus the way I've heard Joe-Joe say it, which is: how-leh.

"No." I respond. Please don't make me say it. *He's looking at me. I know he wants to hear it.* "He called me new boy." I finally mutter.

"Did he say it in a derogatory way?" Dad is unnecessarily interested. He didn't seem to care as much when the kids called me, 'brownie,' 'pineapple' and, 'black mutt' back home.

I shake my head. *Embarrassing.*

"Mom wants us to go to counseling again. Do you know that?" He's sitting forward in his chair, staring at me with accusing eyes.

"Sorry." I murmur. I don't know what else to say.

"Yeah well. Look. I might as well tell you right now before this stuff gets out of hand. About that conversation we were having this morning…" a glazed look washes over his face and I watch as he positions himself so he can peer over my shoulder. A tremendously goofy grin spreads across his face as he waves at my Aunty Jo who is dropping a cooler into the trunk of her car.

I try to get his attention again. "Dad. You were saying?"

He doesn't hear a single word that I say. "What's up, Jo." His face is flush and he's waving at her like he thinks he's my age.

She smiles and sashays in our direction. "Hey Gav, how are you?" she leans down to hug my dad and strokes his back with her press-on fingernails.

"I'm good." He says, holding on to her. "You've been working out. You look good."

"Thank you. You should come work out with me." She says, and pats his legs. "But you have to try and walk for me first."

I roll my eyes and then study Mom's older sister, try to see her from Dad's point of view but it's hard because she looks just like Mom, only skinnier. Same face, same hair color, same eyes, only her personality is the complete opposite. I know Mom and she would never get plastic surgery or wear tiny bikini tops outside of the house or flirt with somebody else's husband. But here Aunty Jo was, letting it all hang out. "How's Haunani? Is she doing better?"

Dad's eyes never lift themselves off of my aunt. "Yeah, she's making progress. You know, sort of taking it one day at a time I guess."

Making progress? Ha! Those words flash through my mind like the punch line of a joke. In reality, Mom is nothing more than a shell of a woman who spends her days talking to

115

Makena's dust, smelling Makena's old clothes, using Makena's blankets, and staring endlessly at Makena's pictures while crying nonstop. If that's making progress, I don't even want to know what making regress looks like.

Should it bother me that Dad's eyes are so focused on my Aunty, that he's smiling, even laughing again when Mom is just a few feet away drowning in the darkness? I look at the front door to our house, contemplate going in but I don't because it seems like Mom's got a problem with me and I don't want to make it worse.

I look back at Dad, whose hands are resting on Aunty Jo's legs. He's telling her he's going to try to walk again, he's going to try physical therapy so he can get in a canoe with her and I shake my head. "Whatever." I'm surprised how one word can stop a whole conversation.

"So how's about it, Gabriel?" She puts her arm around my shoulder and ruffles my hair in a way only reserved for my own mom. "Are you almost ready to go?"

I pull away from her firm grasp and fold my hands over my chest. "Yeah. We should go." I don't know what else to say to her, I mean she's nice and all, and she did take me to school and then pick me up when I was in trouble but I still don't know anything about my aunty except that she seems to like my dad a lot—more than Mom, even.

She pulls me in for a hug and wraps her arms around me. "You're so cuddly."

Gross. Get off of me, old lady. I pull away and step behind Dad. "You want me to help you back in the house?" I ask him.

He throws me a sharp look—the kind that's meant to say,

'let me be, I'm not crippled,' and furrows his brows. "Actually Gabriel I think I'm going to stay out here."

"Fine." I say and stand there, guarding him like a sentinel.

"Maybe you should get a towel." Aunty Jo purrs.

"Naw, I'm fine." I tell her. "I'll just dry off in the sun."

"Go get a towel, Gabe." Dad barks into Aunty Jo's hefty, half naked chest.

I reluctantly walk away and stomp back into the house to get a towel. It's quiet like a tomb and it makes me nervous so I run as quickly as I can to my room. My plan is to get in and get out without making a sound but I must be making a lot of noise because out of the darkness comes Mom's voice. "Gavin?" I try to ignore it, but it's calling out again. "Gavin?"

I tiptoe towards my parent's room where my mother, in her depressed state is resting. *Are you even alive, or is that your ghost talking?* "Dad's outside." I use my indoor voice. It doesn't come out right; sounds more like sprinklers hissing so I clear my throat and begin again. "Mom, Dad's outside with Aunty Jo."

Her head turns toward me sharply, but she doesn't say anything. In the dark her face is scary. She looks like a zombie, pale and skinny and the dark circles under her eyes, and alongside her cheeks make her look authentically ghastly. I cling to the frame of the door out of fear; I don't know if I should leave her when she looks like this but I want so desperately to get out and do something. *I'm going to wither away in here.*

"I was uh— I was going to go with Aunty to meet Grandma and Grandpa at the beach for paddling." I inform her. "Do you—do you want to come?"

"Your Dad going?" She's asking.

117

I don't really know the answer to that—I can't imagine that there are many wheelchair friendly beaches around so I answer, "no."

"Then no." She answers.

I sigh hard, and mutter, "typical."

"What did you just say?" Mom snaps, her voice is stronger than she looks. "Gabriel Kane Foster. What did you just tell me?"

I sigh again and roll my eyes. I'm feeling brave because it's so dark; I know she can't see me. "Nothing."

"You said, 'typical.' What do you mean by that?"

Basically, what I'm saying is that you've become a troll, locked away in a dark corner of the world and that you only come out to eat, poop, and growl at me. "It's nothing." I mutter.

"Gabriel." Mom's voice sounds like it's coming out of severely pursed lips. "Don't make me ask you again."

"I just— I mean— you never want to go anywhere anymore. That's it. At least Dad goes and sits outside. He's sitting out there now." *Putting moves on Aunty Jo…*

"So what." Mom says. That's not a question. "Did you talk to your Dad yet?"

I nod, remember that she probably can't see me— unless she's grown mole eyes, which is possible— and add, "yeah."

"Good." she says, and swishes her hand towards the door. "Go."

I open it and let the light in. For the first time in a while I get a good look at her and can't help but feel worried. Her skin is so pale she could pass for a ghost and because she's carrying the jar-o-Makena again, she could probably attract them too.

118

I head outside to where the bright sun lives. Dad is still out there, but this time, he's talking to the woman that they called, 'Aunty Vai' from the other night. Her arms are folded in front of her chest, and she's glaring down hard at Dad as I'm walking out. He's slumped down in his chair, looking like he wishes he could run away to somewhere far. I wish he could too, because as much as I don't like him right now, I'd go too. I'd rather join him then be here. She turns her head to look at me, slaps my Dad hard on the right side of his face, and walks towards Aunty Jo's car.

I run to Dad but he shoos me away with such a vicious scowl, I swear he thinks I'm an enemy in his war.

My feet divert the rest of me to where Aunty Jo is sitting, and I peer inside. Just U'i, and Mirry. Joe-Joe, George, the younger kids, and our Grandparents are nowhere to be found. "You ready, babes?" Aunty Jo flashes a bright white smile at me. I wonder if the teeth are fake too.

I open the back right door and slide in behind U'i and next to Mirry, who sticks her tongue out at me like a little kid. "Oh grow up." I mumble and stare at Dad. His gaze is fixed on the short green grass in front of our pathway that connects us to everyone else.

"Wait for me. I'm coming." The woman who slapped Dad says, and opens the front passenger door.

"Oh heller. Yeah!" Aunty Jo says. "Fun! This will be awesome. Just like old times again. U'i, go sit in the back with your cousins."

U'i grabs her things and crawls over everything to get between Mirry and me. *Haven't you ever heard of the door?*

Mirry taps the woman on the shoulder and says, "Mom. What happened with you and Uncle Gavin?"

Mom. That explains a LOT.

"Yeah, Aunty Vai. Tell us what happened." U'i demands.

"No respect." She snaps, making sure her voice is as loud as it can be. "Some people just get no respect."

Aunty Jo opens her mouth, like she's ready to protest and then she shuts it again, clamping her top teeth to her bottom lip to prevent any verbal thoughts from escaping. No one says anything as she pulls out of the driveway. Even the stereo gives us the silent treatment as we ride together through the gates of my grandparent's estate.

TWELVE

It's a fifteen-minute drive and Aunty Jo is trying to turn it into an hour by jabbering non-stop to that mean Aunty Vai lady about this person and that; she's even telling jokes that don't make sense to me. Things like, "what did the Hawaiian termite say to the other Hawaiian termite? Eh brah, you like come eat my house?" I play along and laugh with everyone else in a fake 'I'm-freaking-having-fun way but in reality, I'm just too weirded out by my day to really pay attention.

"Oh Gabey, Aunty forgot to tell you that you're riding in one genuine podagee car. You know why dat is?" She pulls into her prime 'lifeguard only' stall, throws the gear into park and smiles in the mirror at me. "It goes 'Pacheco-Pacheco-Pacheco-Pacheco, try listen." She pulls the key out and sure enough, it coughs, 'Pacheco-pacheco-pacheco' before it completely conks out. U'i groans at her joke and jumps out of the old four-door with her left hand shielding her face.

Mirry gets out and waits for me to exit so she can slap me hard in the middle of my back. "You didn't get it did you? A Podagee is a Portuguese. It's funny yeah?

I grinned broadly and nod my head like some dumb talking horse. "Oh, I get it now." I don't. But I would rather pretend I did so I'm not left out of their island humor. *I'm going to prove to everyone here that I'm not a coconut.*

"Nevahmind him, waste time lose money." Joe-Joe comes out of nowhere and flips the back of his hand upward at us. "Come on, Miriam. Joella- we go."

Mirry runs to his side and U'i just stands there, eyes narrowed. "Eh, kuli your mouth Joe-Joe, I told you that I don't like when people call me that." She tilts her head up at me and smiles. "I hate my name, so ug. I like U'i better." She looks at me and flips her hair back like a fail shampoo commercial. "It means beautiful in Hawaiian."

I'm trying to force my eyes to stay normal but I can feel them growing bigger. I squeeze them tight and open them up again; it's hard for me to see my cousin as attractive at all. If anything, she was just like Makena. In fact, I think she might even look like her. I have to check the pictures. She's waiting for me to say something in response but I can't. Mom always says if I can't say something nice…

The rest of our cousins are running towards the beach but she's still rambling on. "Everybody who loves me calls me U'i."

A group of guys walks by and waves at her. "Hi U'i."

She waves back and Aunty Jo catches it. She digs her vicious glare into my cousin. "Who was that?"

"Da kine dem." Her skin looks sweaty as she grabs two paddles from the trunk. She hands me a dinged up one made of wood and hangs on to the nicer paddle with the black oar. "You know, they paddle boys eighteen."

"Boy's eighteen!" Auntie Jo reaches over and slaps Uʻi's muscular leg. "Uh-hum. They're eighteen, huh?" She cups her hands over her mouth to broadcast her voice. "Eh- hui, you two eighteen year olds. You like meet my fists? Talk to Uʻi again, try!"

"Oh my God!" Uʻi grabs my t-shirt and hides behind me. "So shame, Mom!"

"What you guys waiting for? Go." Aunty Vai barks and we run towards the coconut trees where a group of canoes are sitting.

Joe-Joe sees us and smirks. When we get close enough to the circle of kids, he slips in beside me, and points to the smallest coconut tree. "Right there your home. See, dea you." He points at a tiny green oval thing up in the branches.

I figure if I can take on some kid at school I can handle Joe so I shove him as hard as I can. He doesn't go flying like I expected but he does come at me—hard. "What's up, punk?" He pushes me right back. Everyone is moving away from us until we are standing in the middle of a circle.

"Beef, beef, beef!" They're muttering.

From the corners of my eyes, I can see my grandparents on the left side outside of the circle, and my Aunties on the right. I put my forearms up to cover my face just in case Joe-Joe wants to strike.

I close my eyes and feel forceful hands on my shoulders. I blindly swing and feel my right hand connect with a chin. "Braddah you bettah check yo'self befo' you wreck yo'self." The voice growls. That's not my cousin's voice. I slowly open my eyes and see Uncle Nalu. *I'm dead. I am so dead.* He wraps one arm around me and drags me down the beach. *So embarrassing.* I see everyone looking at me and I fight hard to run away. I would rather run than have all those kids see me like this but Uncle is too strong. We get to the edge of the water and he stops when we're ankle high. "You need to cool off, panty." He says and flings me hard into the ocean.

I feel so stupid flailing around in knee deep water. I don't need to look up at any of the other kids; I can hear them laughing. I sit there and glare at him. He reaches down and scoops water into my face. He thinks he's dousing the fire inside of me but he's only fanning the flames. My hands sift around in the sand and I find a white rock the size of my fist.

"What you gonna do?" Uncle Nalu growls, eyeing what I have in my hand. "You try hit me wit' dat. I dare you. You going jail brah. I going lock you up."

"Pfft." I sneer. "*You* are going to lock *me* up? I don't think so."

"Das right, brah." Uncle snaps. "I *will* personally lock you up for assaulting a police officer."

He's a po-po. I stop. Drop the rock. Roll backwards into the arms of the water. It embraces me and I want to cry. *Don't cry don't you dare cry you wuss. Be a man.* I manage to hold it back but it feels like a hard boulder pressing down in my chest.

"Get up." Uncle Nalu barks. "Go by your team."

I don't have a team. I don't move.

"Get up 'fore I whoop you." He snaps.

Police brutality. I stand and trudge through the sand towards the group. *Abuse of power.* There are kids my age, kids who are older than me, and a few who are younger staring in my direction. I can feel myself shrinking as I get closer and closer to them. By the time I reach them, my chin is cutting into my chest. "Sorry." I say to Grandpa.

He frowns at me and for the first time, I feel like he wishes I wasn't his grandson. I look at Grandma. *Does she even know what's been going on? Probably not.* She looks even more disappointed than when I accidentally knocked the baby birds out of her tree. But Aunty Vai is definitely not happy. She's shaking her head and whispering into Aunty Jo's ear.

The other kids are nudging each other and cocking their heads towards me. I try not to look at their faces but my eyes catch a few of them anyway. I see Joe-Joe laughing with two other guys, Georgie making faces at me like a two-year-old, Mirry with her head in the air, pretending she doesn't know me, U'i huddling with her hott friend Napua, and a boy with a very prominent and very fresh black eye. I wince and flick my tongue out to taste the dried blood on my own lip. *He's the boy I wailed on this morning. I know he is.*

"Circle up." Grandpa says. We do as he tells us and he takes a long pause before talking again. "Many of you have been paddling wit' Na 'Ihe for long time, an' we all know dat we no like pi-li-ki-a ovah hea. No matter who you are we no accept negativity inside dese hea boats. Dat means no swearing, no name calling, an' no bad feelings against each oddah when we practice because den it lowers our spirits which in turn affects our performances as a team, an' dis brings more negativity into da canoes. Dese boats, whether oh not you believe it have life in dem. Dey have mana. An' dese boats work like you an' me. You give him strong, positive energy, he go strong. You give him bad energy, he break down. An' let me tell you, once its broken, it's hard to bring it back together. Not impossible, but hard. So what we going do today is some bonding. You guys all gonna run togeddah all da way to da end of da park past Haleʻiwa or what some of you kids nowadays call Aliʻi. Pass dat, go to Kai-a-ka, turn around an' come back.

Everybody groans but me. I have no idea where he means so I don't say a thing.

"Eh, no ack." Grandpa shouts over the noise. The other kids are looking at me as if I am solely to blame and Grandpa adds, "dis not only da new kid's fault. Give some big mahalos to da instigator—da antagonizer of da group too. Dass, right I seen you Joseph. I know you t'ink I blind 'cuz I'm old but I saw. Hopefully dis run going shake all da hewa out yo' bodies and if we lucky, da air you folks breathe will give you renewed life. So go." He yells. "Go fo' one run, an' smile, soak 'em up, have fun. It's a beautiful day."

I follow the group to the street and walk with them until we reach the end of the short rock wall. The air that is coming off the black asphalt feels like an oven and the smell that is coming off of my skin is like baked nacho chips. *Great. I'm cooking.* A few kids up ahead start picking up the pace and we all mimic them until we're all jogging.

We go through the Ana-hu-lu bridge we drove over the first day we touched down on the island; where the kids were fishing and the girls in the half bikini bottoms were walking, down the path that forks off to the right. We keep on running. Past a harbor filled with boats, past half-empty parking lots, past huge grassy fields, a church, some houses on the left hand side, some dorks on the right.

My gut is twisting into my side by the time we reach the place with a sign that reads, '*Kaiaka*' but no one is stopping. They turn right around and start running back to Grandpa. I'm working on my breathing but my side hurts too badly for me to keep up the pace so I slow down to a walk. I'm panting now and I can see the majority of the kids getting smaller and smaller as they run ahead past the field weirdos and the parking lot. Another kid slows down up ahead. I catch up with him, swallow hard and say, "Hey. Thanks for waiting for me. I'm Gabe." I look at him. It's the kid I punched in the face this morning.

"John." He says. We walk together for a long time. I concentrate on how I feel so I don't have to talk to him but I can't stop thinking about how stupid I was for wailing on him for no good reason. *Talk to him. Tell him something. Tell him sorry or something. Jesus Christ, Gabriel you at least owe him that.* "Look." I whisper through dried out lips. He turns and blinks at me. "About today."

"Whatevah." John pants. "I'm used to getting beat up anyway."

Now I feel worse. *Tell him you went berserk on him because of your cousins. Better yet, tell him it's because of your sister. You know you want to; Makena is the whole reason why everything in your life is screwed up right now. If she was still alive you'd be in this thing together—you wouldn't be going through this wretched life alone and you never would've hit him.* "Man." *Is that all you can say, Gabe?* But all I can think to say is, "Man, I'm sorry man."

Stupid.

He doesn't say anything, just lets it roll off his back. We pick up our feet after we reach the harbor and jog in silence back to the canoe site.

"All hands on da boat." Grandpa orders once the two of us reach the rest of them, and we surround the canoe. When every one of us is touching the boat, he continues. "You feel da mana? Da power in dis circle?" Some people nod. *Liars. I feel nothing but hot breath and gooey arms touching me.* "Dis goodness that you feel comes from the goodness inside all of you. It's from working togeddah wit' one common goal an' dat goal is to: I mua. To move forward. When we are united we are all ikaika. Strong. Now, e pule kakou."

We all bow our heads and listen to his prayer. "Lord, thank you for blessing us with your light today and every other day. " He coos in his best English. "Mahalo also, for giving us the ability to learn humility, and cooperation, and for bringing peace within our paddling 'ohana. Let us be ever mindful of the feelings of others, and let us have peace and respect towards one another. I humbly ask that we have a good practice today and that you keep all of your keiki; your beautiful children right here in front of me, safe as they go out to sea, and that you keep them safe as they make their journeys home. We humbly ask that you please bless those who cannot be with us today and guide them back to us when they're good and ready. In Jesus name we pray."

"Amene," we answer when he's finished.

Joe-Joe walks over to me, throws his sweating, muscular arm over my shoulder and gives me a noogie. It feels like he's pretending, like he's trying to look good in front of everyone else but I'm too tired to strangle him with my (soon to be) muscular fingers, so I stand there and let my shoulder, and neck soak up his armpit juice. I mean, I smell so bad already, I figure what's a little more meaty cheese stench added to my nacho chips aroma? "I ku maumau!" He yells in my ear.

"I ku wa!" The other kids respond.

"I ku mau mau, I ku huluhulu I ka lana wau!" Joe-Joe thrusts his chest upwards into my face.

"I ku wa!" The other kids scream with excitement.

"I ka lana wau!" Joe-Joe bellows.

"I ku wa!" The other kids sing and then altogether they chant, "I ku wa huki, I ku wa kou I ku wa'a mau e mau kai hulu, e huki e, kulia!"

Another kid starts up again and they do it all over again so that by the third and final round, even *I* am feeling feverish. "Cheehoo!" They all scream as the last words come out. I have no clue what they were chanting but I'm caught up in it and add a quiet little, "whoo!" in there too. Grandpa is grinning at us with approval and points his finger at the boat and the ocean. We all grab a section near each seat and lift the canoe.

"'A'ohe hana nui ke ahu 'ia," he yells at us from behind, "Many hands make heavy work light."

We walk the canoe over to the ocean's edge and set it in until the rear is floating on the surface, and then we get another boat, and another, and another until all the boats we need are in the water.

U'i grabs my paddle when she grabs hers, and she hands it to me. I stand between her and Napua and try to concentrate on whatever is being said by whoever looks important. I glance over at Napua with the side of my eye. White bikini top, striped rainbow surf shorts, hair in two braids. Nice. Grandpa begins calling out seats. "Joe-Joe come steer this one. Georgie, one. John, two…"

One by one everyone drops into his or her seat and I wait and wait patiently for coach Grandpa to call my name but he doesn't. "Warm up to the buoy and back." He tells them, and they take off. I stand there like a doof and dig my paddle into the sand. "Gabriel," he says to me, "I like you go out wit' Nalu."

I reel backwards. *I don't want to go anywhere with him! The dude hates me, he hates me!*

And just like he's on cue, Uncle Nalu walks past us balancing a smaller canoe on his head. It's sleek, shiny, and black with glitter paint that makes it look like endless amounts of stardust was dumped all over it. He puts it down on the ground the way one would set down a baby, and walks back up the beach. "No." I blurt out to Grandpa.

"What you said?" Grandpa's hands drop on his hips.

"No?" I say again, and look up at Grandpa with my extra cute face in hopes that he will change his mind. The face worked for Makena all the time, why shouldn't it work for me too?

"I no t'ink so." He says in his normal accent. "I nevah give you one choice. You no can say 'no' to me. I da boss. I da big whip. Only t'ing I like hear coming out from dat mout' of yaws is yes, coach. You heard?"

"Yeah."

"Yeah what?"

"Yeah—coach?" My dog face is broken.

Uncle Nalu walks by us again with another canoe. He drops that one into the sand and I feel relieved that at least I won't have to sit in the same canoe as him. Until I see that the one he's urging me to stand by is bright, and bubblegum pink with metallic, rainbow colored stars all over it.

THIRTEEN

"What. What's your problem?" Uncle Nalu asks, eyeing me up and down.

I shrug. How can I tell him that *he* is my problem?

"Eh, whatevah. You like paddle." He barks. "Go get yo' paddle."

My feet sink until the sand is up to my shins but I hurry as fast as I can to claim my borrowed paddle. I guess someone put it next to the tree where Aunty Jo and Aunty Vai are sitting. The two aren't saying anything to each other but I feel like I'm interrupting something anyway. I look over at them and force a smile. I must look like I'm trying to cover up a fart because they give each other a look and get up to move their chairs back. Uncle Nalu looks pissed so I grab my paddling tool and tread back down through the sand to where he is waiting.

"Wa'a." He says, using the 'v' sound and gesturing at his black, sparkly man-looking boat. "Noho, pikao, manu ihu, kuamo'o, mo'o, manu hope, 'iako, ama," he's pointing all over the place and I'm so lost.

I guess he sees that I am nowhere to be found so he stops and frowns. "Noho," he points to the seats. "Pikao," he runs his hands along the sleek body of the boat. "Manu ihu," he walks to the front of the boat and holds onto the nose— the tip of the canoe. "Kuamoʻo," he pats the bottom of the boat. "Moʻo" his fingers trace the line going across the side of the boat until he's at the back next to me. "Manu hope," he holds the tip at the back end of the boat. "An' here's your ʻiako," he pats the two arms that go crossways and reach out to the ocean, just like Dad described it on the plane that day we flew in, "an' dat's your ama." He gently taps the outrigger float with his bare toe. "You can remembah dat?" I nod stiffly, and he laughs. "Chyeah right."

"Ama," I say, and gently point at the floater with my toe, "'iako," I pat the arms that stretch across, "uh that's a manu something."

"Yeah I thought so," he says and laughs.

I'm not a coconut. "Manu ihu, I think, and a manu hopi?"

"Ho-peh." He nods. "And?"

"Uh, the oʻo and the pika?"

"Moʻo and the pikao, close." Uncle uncrosses his hands from his chest and looks at me like, *continue.*

"Okay ah, kua...moʻo?" I tap the bottom of the boat, "noho?" I pat the seat with my open palm, "and waʻa?" I gesture at the entire canoe with two hands.

"Vaʻa." He corrects my pronunciation and pats me on the back. "Okay, maikaʻi. Good. Good." He grabs his paddle, and shakes his head. "I'm surprised. You did bettah than I expected. Maybe you turn out good like us yet." He stands upright and is back to business again. "Anyways, dis is called a hoe. Say it wit' me. Ho-eh."

"Ho-ay." I repeat.

"Ho-EH." He says, gruffly.

"Ho-EH?"

He nods. "Here's how you hold yo' hoe," he says and positions his hands on his paddle. His right hand is gripping a T-top handle that fits just inside his closed fist, and his left hand is firmly squeezing what Uncle calls the, 'kuʻau.' It's a shaft that rests just above the, 'palaulau,' which is the fat, teardrop-shaped blade that pulls the water. The *oar* as we would call it back home.

I mimic his hand positions and he raises his eyebrows at me. *Finally, I'm doing something right. He's impressed. And that he should be.*

"Braddah," he hisses and laughs. "You get da t'ing going backwards." I look down at the blade. *I can't tell if it's forward or backward, I can't help it if I've never seen or held one of these things before, especially since it looks nothing like a kayak paddle or a real oar, which are things I've seen at least. Duh!* Uncle grabs the paddle away, turns it around so the rounder part and the logo are facing front, shoves it back in my hands. "Dea. You feel dat?" I nod. "Da ʻupe, da flat part goes in back, da palaualau or da sticker part shows up front. See? Advertisement." He points to his paddle. It reads:

HOE HEKILI

"No can scoop wit' da rounded area, the round part no can pull water so we pull wit' da opposite side. Jus' like yo' hands. Your palms flat, or round?"

"Round." I answer without thinking.

"Brah you must be mutant then ʻcuz my palms are flat."

I smile for the first time at him. "I meant flat."

"Yeah, right. Kay. So when you swim da flat part of yo' hand grabs da water yeah? Wait—you do know how for swim, yeah?" Uncle yells. *His voice is so danged loud; doesn't he come with volume control?*

"Yup." I say as enthusiastically as I can even though I never actually swam in the ocean before and even though I'm kind of scared of what is lurking beneath the surface, and even though I hate the smell of fish and crab. I shudder at the thought of falling in. In fact, I'm deathly scared. And yet I lie. Why? Because I'm not into the functional application of my body parts when it hits the water at this point, I just want to fast-forward this part so I can paddle and show everyone that I can do what Dad says Mom used to do. *Maybe if they see me doing something that's a big part of their lives, they'll learn to like me.*

Uncle grabs the manu ihu—the nose of the wa'a, *oh yeah I'm so impressive* and I help him by lifting the manu hope—the backside of his canoe so it doesn't scrape across the rocks. It's no heavier than Dad's wheelchair and I have no doubts that I can lift it by myself just like Uncle Nalu did.

We walk it out until the canoe is waist deep and he takes the backseat in the boat. "Kay. Think of yo' paddle like it's an extension of you. Da ka'au—da shaft is like yo' arm, an' da palaulau—da blade is like yo' hand. Remembah what I told you about yo' hand. Kay. Hold da canoe."

I hold the front of the canoe and he raises his arms with his hands in the same position on the paddle as they were in earlier. Left hand on the handle, right hand gripping the shaft.

"I going learn you da triangle." He sits upright like a

pigeon: chest puffed up head high. He leans forward a little, twists his torso to the left, drops his right shoulder, puts his right foot forward, and takes a stroke in the water on his right side. His blade cuts through the surface of the water like the scissors Makena once chopped all of my hair off with. *Reverse mohawks are the style she said. It'll be fun, she said. But what she didn't say is that I would look like Bozo (who was supposed to be Makena's future boyfriend) and that random people on the street would start giving me money because after Mom got through with me (she said she was trying to fix it) the whole world thought I was a cancer patient. (I wound up donating the money to people who had actual cancer even though I wanted to by a game console because one of my Mom's 'friends' said it wasn't funny and threatened that she was going to report us to the police.)*

Uncle Nalu is frowning at me. He leans forward, twists, digs his paddle into the ocean and pulls it back mid thigh. The boat leers forward and knocks me right into the water. The salty ocean feels good all over my charred body—but it stings my eyes and frightens me at the same time; sort of like Mom's cooking. I stand up and blindly reach for the canoe. When my head emerges, Uncle Nalu is laughing at me. "Sorry ah, boy. I guess I don't know my own strength."

I'm strong too, I just wasn't prepared that's all. "No, I *wanted* to get in there." I say and hold the canoe's front again. This time, I shove my feet in the sand, feel the rounded pieces of coral between my toes, and lean forward to balance myself. *I'm ready for you.* I throw my arm around the manu ihu *whoohoo I'm good* and pull it into my side. I have a pretty firm grasp now; this boat is in a dangerous headlock. *Try knocking me down now.*

He leans forward, explains something about a scalene triangle to me, something about his arms and shoulders making the shape or something. Something about using the core, something about incorporating a twist and reaching and pulling the blade straight up and down next to the gunnels. Something, something, something. I don't know, because I stopped listening. Napua is back.

She's sitting in the first seat so we both have a nice view of each other, and her hair is pulled back and wet. Like she wet it. Or something.

"You watching?" Uncle Nalu snaps.

"Y-yeah." I tell him, eyes still on Napua. *I'm watching. She's waving—is she waving at me?* I lift the arm that is wrapped around the canoe *I'm not cheating on Deanna... waving isn't cheating—or is it?* And wave back just in case—you know—it was meant for me. But just as I do that, Uncle takes a huge pull of water with his paddle and the canoe soars forward and pops me right in the chest. I'm back down in the water on my butt again, flailing my arms around as if I can't swim in two feet. *Great. Now I've really got her attention.*

I stand up and Uncle grabs water with the flat part of his paddle and douses me with it. "Bah, pay attention."

"Yeah," I say, spitting out pieces of hairy looking seaweed, "when do I get a chance?"

"Next time." Uncle says, and jumps off the canoe. He places his paddle on the seats and drags the wa'a back toward the beach.

"I thought I was going to get to go out today." I protest. *It looks like cake. Wait 'til I show Napua what I can do.*

"Well you thought wrong." He says, and walks over to the other canoes.

"Come on."

"What, you like go out? Fine. Get on top." Uncle pulls the boat back to me and gets back on.

I wait until he is talking to someone; I don't want him to bust my chops again. I sneak around to the side without the 'ama and pull myself in. As I'm jumping, the whole boat decides to flip and Uncle hits the water with it.

I can see him flailing around like an idiot under the boat, *is that what I looked like? Wait-- he's not coming up-- maybe he's drowning!* I reach my hand under the wa'a and feel his hand gripping mine. I pull. I can feel him pulling back. I'm trying to use all of my weight but he was right, he *is* much stronger. *I'm going down!* When I'm completely drenched, he lets go and pushes me up. My head is out of the water so I clear my eyes with the backs of my hands and look. Bubbles. More bubbles. And then nothing. I'm trying to find the strength to call for help when someone grabs me from behind.

"Brah!" Uncle Nalu's voice is like really shoddy music to my ear drums. "You gotta get on from da 'ama side. Always get up by da 'ama or you going turn everyone over. Hawaiian term fo' when da boat flips is huli. You huli da boat out there an' dats it. Pau. Over. And what you t'ink you doing, anyway? Trying for steal my boat. Yours is pink-unicorn-sparkles my braddah. She was *made* fo' you. Go get her and bring her back here."

I hate that he calls that thing a her. I pull myself out of the water, and lurch like a heavy rat toward the stupid pink boat. I lift it up. It feels like a whale. I want to kick it down the beach but because Uncle is looking at me *and only because he's looking at me* I nicely hoist it over my head and wear it like a dumb pink umbrella hat down to the shoreline.

Clumps of sand are aiming for my eyeballs as I walk it to hip level. I let it down *carefully because he's still looking at me* and let it float.

I climb up on the side that the 'ama and the 'iako's are on. *I am not flipping over again.* The boat feels tippy and I'm trying to balance myself so I'm on straight. Uncle Nalu turns and looks at me over his left shoulder and signals with his head that I follow him. *Was it an isosceles triangle? Or an acute triangle that I'm supposed to recreate?* We paddle to the left and head straight out until everything below us is dark blue. My stomach starts to turn. *What happens if I fall in?*

FOURTEEN

In a perfect world, I would have taken off like a bullet through the water and shown everyone who the best paddler in the family really is. Mom would have been right there with me acting normal— at least long enough to stand up and cheer me on, Dad would have ran barefooted to the shoreline, his mouth full of apologies for wishing I'd never been born, Makena would have tears in her eyes for *me*, and heaps of praise to give out instead of the other way around, and my Uncle would give me his boat because as he'd say, he's, *not worthy of riding it*, but my world is so far from being perfect that of course, only the worst things imaginable could possibly happen.

Yes, I flipped.

Again, and again and oh yes, again.

I flipped right in front of Napua (repeatedly) in front of the kid I accidentally but not so accidentally smashed in the face, in front of my dumb cousins, in front of the Aunties, in front of the grandparents, in front of the whole entire beach.

And each time I would try to get back on, my chest would

tighten so that I could barely get any breath out of my throat and because I'm such a klutz I'd climb on only to fall right back off again. But that wasn't the bad thing.

The bad thing was that Uncle Nalu neglected to teach me how to steer his stupid Pink unicorn sparkles boat so I had to figure it out by myself. There were two pedals under each of my feet and when I stepped on the left one, the canoe veered to the left. When the right one was pressed, I'd go off to the right. Easy enough, except that I must've pumped my foot down too hard— or too many times on the right side because the dumb pedal got stuck and wouldn't release. And when I stepped on the left side, that one got stuck too.

I started floating, floating, floating away; far out to where the water under me was so dark, a flashlight couldn't brighten it up.

The theme song from *Jaws* started playing in my mind. So what do I do? I fall again because the boat is tippy and I'm *so* lucky. But this time, I somehow kick the boat away and it sails off into the opposite direction that I fall in and it's escaping me fast. I struggle to swim to it but my arms are sore from paddling, my legs are cramping from pedaling my feet to keep my head alive, and the waves are pulling me backwards so I'm moving deeper into the blackness. I could see the stupid pink boat taunting me, could see Uncle Nalu's shoulders and arms doing that stupid *is it a right triangle?* Movement, could imagine jagged teeth directly under me, and for a fleeting moment, I thought, *this is it. I'm going to die. Here is where I'll meet up with Makena.*

I felt my head going under; *should I even bother swallowing air?* I did, but I don't know why. I guess my lungs must have figured they'd just prolong the inevitable, and the rest of me kicked back and waited for the scenes from my measly little life to play. As I sank deeper and deeper into the abyss below, I realized that I was no longer wondering *or* worrying about whether a shark was going to come, or whether or not fish and eels were swimming all around. I felt relaxed. The water around me was cold and it was only getting colder.

It's about then that I learned that your body does dumb stuff when you feel like you've made up your mind to surrender. I know this now because mine fought hard against giving up. My arms, my legs, my toes were cramping and yet, they all worked together to get me to the surface and in my mind, I could see her face— my sister— Makena smiling down at me, leading me towards my parent's bedroom light like she did when we were smaller.

'Come here, Gabey,' Her eyes seemed to be saying. I was four years old again, lost, and frightened because I'd had a nightmare and she was going to take me back to Mom and Dad. Her hand reached for me, and I went to her. I remember thinking that for the first time since the accident, I could remember everything about her. The way she looked, talked, walked, dressed, smelled. Like powdered armpits and prissiness. I even remembered the way she smiled at me when she was being authentically nice. *I'm coming to be with you,* I thought, *just a second, Makena, I'm almost there.*

Right when I thought that, I felt something large beneath my feet. *There it is. This is goodbye. Adios, sayonara, aloha.* Whatever the thing was bumped me hard, just as my last bit of breath was used up—nudged me so roughly that my face was up above the surface, and I was breathing.

Just as I popped up, someone else dropped in beside me. I closed my eyes, to keep the water out and expected to see the behemoth of a thing that pushed me upwards, or worse, Uncle Nalu frowning at me. When I opened my eyes again, I saw a face I had never seen before. A dude's face.

"Boy, you alright?"

I nodded, and instinctively reached out for his board. I was dying from all that water treading I was doing. He pushed it closer to me so I could grab onto it and gave me a polite smile; you know, the kind where the corners of the mouth lift up but none of the teeth show? "Thanks." I sputtered, and rested my head against the board. I felt so exhausted.

"Bah, I seen you from ovah deah," The man was kicking backwards, positioning himself so that he could get back on his paddle board, and moving his head to point out the area he was stalking me from. "I saw erryt'ing. I was watching you on what, is that your honey's boat?"

I cringed, thinking of Uncle Nalu— the true owner of the boat— as any kind of honey anything. "Ugh. No way. Dude. It's— it belongs to my Uncle."

"Oh." He said but his eyes called me a liar. He must've seen me make some weird expression because he started adding an explanation right away. "Nah, no worries, I have one Uncle who's li' dat too."

I started laughing and my mouth did one of those sounds that sound like I was ripping paper, but I didn't care. I wondered what Uncle Nalu would have said if he heard someone insinuate that he was gay, but I didn't tell the dude that he wasn't. Let him believe that, I don't know him.

"Get on," I remember him saying, "you go in the front, and I'll paddle you from the back."

"How's about I paddle you?" I said, climbing up on the board. It was green and black, and a lot wider than the stupid pink sparkle unicorn canoe—plus, it had this really cushy black padding that felt good under my fingers and toes.

"No fricken way."

"Why not?" I asked him.

He climbed up behind me. "Brah. No ways. I seen da damage you did out dea already. You nuts if you think I going to let you flip *me* over and kick *my* board out to da open sea."

He talked a lot with his hands, so the board was rocking with him on it. I was scared we were going to tip over again, so I asked if we could switch so that he was paddling in the front and I was hanging on in the back.

"Okay but you bettah not check out my butt da whole time I'm standing up and paddling." He said, in a playful tone. "I don't even know you."

"I don't know you either," I smiled.

"I'm Ikaika." He sassed. "So now you know me." The boat started moving as soon as he dipped his paddle in the water.

"I'm Gabe." I was trying not to stare at his hairy back and his skinny butt crack— I mean, I couldn't help but look up at it a few times; I was sitting down and he was standing, his surf shorts were falling off, and it was only in my face.

"What, nice, da view?" He snapped, and furrowed his bushy brows at me.

I looked the other way. *Crack is whack.*

"Dea." He said, after a minute of pushing me where the water turned light blue.

"You want me to get off?" I slipped off the boat and let my feet dangle. I looked at him again, but this time, I stared directly into his face. I don't know why, but I felt like I was like I was staring at Makena.

"Brah, you nuts." He panted, and used his paddle to point in the direction of something wooden and long floating around in the water. "Get back on da board. I don't even think you can swim."

"I can swim," I answered, in defense of myself. "I'm just not used to swimming in… in…"

"In water?" He cracked back and jumped in to the ocean, feet first. "Wait here." He bossed, and added, "put your feet down so you don't just float away from me." He turned around, swam to my Grandpa's paddle, then brought it back to me. "Here." He handed the end with the T-handle to me. "Now let's go get your, ahem, Uncle's boat."

"Thanks," I told him, and made room for him to get back on with me again. "And it *is* my Uncle's boat because I wouldn't ever choose a color like that." I felt that needed to be said because it seemed like he was accusing me of choosing that paint job.

"Brah, it's okay." Ikaika muttered, "I know, I know how it is."

"You know how *what* is?" I asked.

"Nothing," he sputtered, and laughed.

And for some reason, maybe because of the same dumb reflex I had when my sister died, I laughed too. Laughed until tears came dribbling out of the corners of my eyes. And it felt like the first time I let that noise come out of me in a long time. I was so happy about the laughter that I started to cry like a lunatic.

"Eh, eh." He said, and sat down behind me. "Gabe. Boy. You okay, or what?" I felt his fingers touch my left shoulder and I let them sit there. It felt good to be comforted by someone, even if it was just some stranger on the sea. It felt even better that he didn't yank his hand away, or flip me off the board, or anything that I'd expect from everyone else in my life, he just left his hand there and let me cry.

After a while, I stopped, and I knew I had to say something, but no explanations would come out. "S-s-s-s-orry," My chest heaved until the words popped out of my mouth.

"S'okay." He said, and softly popped me in my chin with his fist. "No need to tell me what happened. I no need know. It's probably none of my business anyway. Main thing is that you're okay now."

The relief I felt after he said that made me want to spew my guts to him, but I didn't. I just couldn't let it go. He paddled us back to shore, but neither of us could see the stupid pink boat anymore.

"Someone must've picked it up." He cooed and jumped off of the board. He was about waist high in the water, so I jumped down to join him. "Maybe your Uncle?"

"Maybe," I said, and studied his face. I remembered thinking that he looked like a kind man. He had these deep brown eyes that I *think* Makena had, framed by long eyelashes that curled slightly at the ends. "I mean, I hope so. My Uncle would never let me hear the end of it." I said, and looked away, because it started getting weird with us just standing so close to shore together. "Thank you." I mumbled, and held my paddle up as I walked towards the beach. "For… for everything."

"'A'ole pilikia." He cooed.

"Huh?"

"Hawaiian way for saying, no problem."

I nodded and walked away from him feeling like I was leaving something behind, but I didn't bother looking back. It was probably better that I didn't, seeing as how he was a stranger who guessed right off the bat that I couldn't swim.

When I got back to the area that my family was sitting, I was surprised to see that no one even seemed to notice that I almost died out there. Both boats were tied onto Grandpa's truck— cosmic beauty *and* stupid pink unicorn sparkles.

"Ho bah," my Uncle's voice came out from somewhere— most likely, the garbage can. "Whea you was?" He picked out a random tourist that was walking around in a less-than string bikini that she was ten sizes too big for. "Picking up chicks?"

I must've been looking at him like I couldn't understand because he started gesturing in the air and talking slower and louder as if I were deaf. People around us started laughing; the kids who were lucky enough to get in the big canoe, my Aunties, my grandparents, my cousins. I looked to the ocean.

"Ho! Look da whale!" It was the same kid. The one who called me niu boy in school. The one who said his name was John, who made that stupid comment. I balled my hands into fists, and stood there while everybody laughed.

"No—" he yelled, "no— I mean, look!" He pointed out toward the area that my— I mean Uncle's boat flipped over and we all saw a big splash in the water.

"Dass not one whale, maka po" Uncle Nalu said, after a few seconds. "That's one nai'a."

"What's a nai'a?" I wondered aloud. *That must've been the thing that was pushing me up out of the deep.*

"Tell boy haole what one nai'a is, Johnny boy." Uncle Nalu said over his shoulder, as he strutted away towards the car.

"Dolphin." John muttered. "It's a dolphin."

Makena. Makena's favorite animal was a dolphin. I wonder if that's her in that guardian form like the hawks…
"What's a— whatever that other word was that he said?" I asked him.

"It means blind." John said, and turned away from me.

"Oh." My eyes drifted back out to the water, not to see the dolphin again *although that was so cool* but to look for Makena.

FIFTEEN

Napua's name means the flowers. I know this because she keeps telling me that's all it means.

"Any specific kind of flower, or just flowers?" I ask.

"Just flowers." She says.

"All flowers in general?" I tease.

"Yes."

"Even the ugly ones?"

"Ugh." She's wrinkling her nose and kneeing me in the thigh. She's so hott when she's pissed off.

"What? I'm just asking." I say. I am so lucky I got stuck in the 'girl car.' Luckier that Napua decided to spend the rest of the week with weird U'i because it means I get to see her around more than I normally do.

She whips out her phone and starts texting with it. *Is she texting a guy? Wait— why do I care? Should I care?* I peek over at her screen. It says 'U'i.' She's texting my cousin. It says one word: Gabriel.

"What?" She catches me checking her phone out. "Stop looking."

I want to know what she's saying but I don't want her getting mad at me again so I sit back a little and lean away from her. I turn my head a little so I'm facing the window but my eyes are reading her screen. *Because I am a ninja.* Now it says: is SO weird.

U'i is laughing from the other side of the car. And now Mirry is leaning over Napua's shoulder and laughing too.

"True!" Mirry snorts. "So true."

If I'm weird they're freakishly abnormal. I frown and stare out the window. *Jerks.* I glance at Napua one last time before we pull into our driveway. *Yeah, she's pretty but who cares because I'm taken. By Deanna. De-a-nna*

Aunty Jo stops the car and I'm the first to jump out. "Thanks, Aunty." I say *because I have manners not like some people.* I open the front door so Aunty Vai can get out and she pushes me out of her way.

Aunty Jo gets out of her car and crows, "wow sis, he good boy, yeah?"

Aunty Vai looks up and gives Aunty Jo a look that clearly says: *are you nuts?*

I shrug and head up the driveway.

"Where are you going?" Aunty Vai snaps. I don't even turn around. *You're not my Mom.* I can imagine her giving Aunty Jo the 'you see what an evil kid he *really* is?' Look.

"To get the mail." I shout over my shoulder, and keep climbing towards the gate.

"Such a good boy, Gabey!" Aunty Jo yells after me.

Woof. I lift my hand to acknowledge her— I don't know what that was… praise? Doggy compliment? And walk faster before she starts giving me orders like: *lie down* or *sit* or *beg*.

I hear giggling behind me, next to me, and then suddenly my dumb cousins and their hott— I better stop calling her that— hott friend take off ahead. "He's waiting for a letter from his haole girl girlfriend," Uʻi's explaining. "She's from California." The way she says it makes me sick. All long and drawn out like Ca-lifffff-orrrrr-nyyye-yayyyyy.

I start running too, pump my arms really fast and lift my feet up high because I heard somewhere *I think it might have been on the Internet* that this move helps to give you speed. It's not working. If anything it's making my shins really sore. So sore, I slow down. I can barely walk now, *stupid guy on the how-to website* so I am forced to stop and have a panic attack while I watch them.

They reach into the metal box and bring out a whole stack of letters.

I want to ask them, *anything for me?* But I know that'll make them more curious so I calmly say, "hey, Mirr—did your ointment come in?"

Mirry reels around and stares at me in horror. "How did you know about my ointment?"

Wait— someone actually had ointment? What are the odds? "Everyone knows about that." I say, using my best innocent child voice. "And everyone knows *exactly* where you put it."

She's looking at Uʻi; giving her the I-can't-believe-you-told-everyone-my-secret-how-could-you glare.

"Yup." I tell Mirry. "Uʻi told me. And she was going around telling everybody at practice too."

"I was not!" U'i is shouting.

We all turn at the sound of squealing brakes, and move out of the way so Grandpa's truck can get through. He stops in front of U'i and rolls his window down. "Eh. Thank you, yeah? Got anything for me?" U'i sorts through the stack of mail and gives him his portion. He pats her on the head and waves at us before making his way down towards his house.

I'm looking at her hands, and notice that she still has one letter. One single, solitary letter. I'm thinking it's for me so I sneak up next to her and make a grab for it. She pulls it away from me and holds it far away from me. "Not so fast, liar."

"What?" I ask. "How did I lie?"

"Let's find out!" She exclaims and rips the letter open.

Is it mine? She drops the envelope on the floor. I look at it, recognize the handwriting, and snatch it up off of the pavement. *It is mine!*

"Give it." I growl.

"No." She says, and clears her throat and starts to read. "Greetings, Gabriel. Greetings Gabriel?" They all laugh.

"I'm serious, *Joella*." My hands feel clammy, and my stomach is dancing to the crazy rhythm of my heart.

"Oh no you didn't." U'i snaps and goes back to reading my letter. "Hey, old friend… old *friend?* Who is this from, someone's grandma?" She's laughing like a donkey and her eyes are drinking up the sweet perfume of my girl's ink without giving me a whiff.

"Give it." I yell.

"Or what?" She sneers.

Uncle Nalu's truck is making it's way towards us, so we

split up. Me on one side of the driveway, them on the other end. I'm so desperate to get my hands on my precious letter. "It's a federal violation to tamper with other people's mail." I inform her.

"So?" Is her retort.

"So you can get arrested." I reply.

"And who's going to do that?" She asks me.

Grrr the girl is just like Makena was. "He is." I yell, and point at Uncle Nalu, who is driving past the four of us.

"Oh yeah?" She shouts, and then runs over to Uncle Nalu's driver's side window. "Uncle, you going arrest me?"

He slams on the brakes and stares at her. "Hah? For what?"

"Opening this." She says, and hands it to him.

His grubby hands are all over the letter— *my letter* now, but his mouth is running. "Greetings, Gabriel. Greetings, Gabriel?" He looks over at me. I shrug and limp over to his truck. "Hey, old friend! Sorry about Malina." Uncle pauses to snort. *"Who's Malina?"* I think he's going to stop, but he squints his eyes and keeps right on going. *"Must be hard to be without a sister. As for me, life is perfect. I just started seeing Brad..."* Uncle Nalu stops reading, and folds the letter up. "Brah."

My eyes are misting over and my face is on fire.

Brad. Who the hell is Brad? I want to rip him apart. How could her life be perfect when I'm not in it? And since when were we just friends? As far as I know I'm still her boyfriend so that means she's cheating on me. How could she do that? I bought her what she wanted, I gave her stuff, I carried her bags, I told her everything. Everything.

I thought we were in love.

I thought she cared about me the way I cared about her.

If we hadn't moved here, none of this would have happened.

She didn't even know my sister's name.

"So much for having a *girlfriend*." Mirry's voice is saying somewhere from behind the fog.

"Kuli, Mirry." Uncle Nalu is using his gentle voice. "Braddah, I-I don't know what fo' say." He sounds like he's right next to me and that's the last place I want him to be.

"Leave me alone." I whisper. *She said the 'F' word to me and started going out with some kook without even breaking it off with me first. It hurts. It hurts, it hurts, it hurts, it hurts, it hurts.*

I feel his callused hand on my right shoulder, feel the folded letter brush against my left forearm. I don't want to take it. I don't want to touch it. It's tainted. Too many eyes have looked at it, too many ears have heard what dumb, greedy faced Deanna had to say, but I am the only one who holds this burden; this grief. I let the stupid paper drop to the ground like a stone. Like my heart. *I waited for nothing.*

I take a few steps, and stop when I hear a high-pitched shriek. A dwarf sized bird with sharp talons and a curved, scissor-like beak swoops down and pecks at the letter. The girls cackle like a bunch of witches. The bird stretches its shiny, bronze wings out and looks at me with serious bird eyes. I gulp and back away as fast as a sloth fearing for its life can go, hoping it won't think to fly at me and claw my face off. Fortunately for me, it doesn't, and instead, rips the letter up on the driveway, cocks its big head, and carries the shredded paper upward towards the branches.

My cousins are still laughing at my misfortune, but as they squawk about what happened to my letter, the bird lets them know what it thinks about them by dropping thick and juicy white nuggets down from the sky. There's something for each of them— one for U'i's arm, one for Mirry's shoe, and some for Napua's head, shoulders, and back.

Uncle Nalu's guffawing as loud as is humanly possible, and hollering, "good for you, see, *hachi*— that's what happens when you act li' dat, bad things happen to you!"

The girls run screaming, because the bird is circling above them but even witnessing a real life angry bird doesn't make me break a smile.

SIXTEEN

When I get home, Dad is nowhere to be found.

Neither is Mom.

What I do find though, is a letter. It's on the empty shelf in the empty refrigerator. It's scratched out in Mom's handwriting and reads:

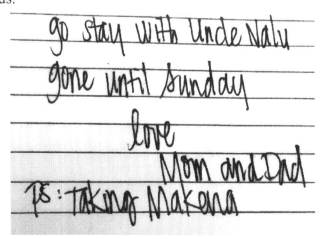

Why didn't they say something to me earlier?

It's so ugly, it hurts my eyes to read, but I think it says:

Go stay with Uncle Nalu. *Not going to happen.* Gone until

Sunday. *Why? What is so important that they have to pick up and leave for two whole days without me?* Love Mom and Dad. *Love. Psshh. Love makes people do really stupid things I guess, like devoting all your time and allowance to a cheating girl who doesn't even love you back, or leaving your kid alone in a house with no food without saying goodbye.* PS: Taking Makena. *Well, lucky her.* I crumple the note, throw it back in the fridge and start opening the cupboards in search of something to eat.

Beans.

Missing parents.

Dead sister.

Friend.

Stupid girls.

Uncle Nalu.

What is wrong with this world?

I don't want to, but considering that Grandpa is probably mad at me, and Grandma is probably ashamed of how I acted at the beach, and seeing as how Aunty Jo has all the weirdos at her house, and that they all reek of hawk poop, and judging by how much Aunty Vai seems to hate me, I do as the note says and head over to Uncle Nalu's house. But only because I'm so hungry, my head is spinning.

If Uncle Nalu is anything like I think he is, I am going to starve. I pull the door closed behind me and sigh.

I hate my life.

SEVENTEEN

Uncle Nalu's house is full. And by that, I mean that he has a lot of kids running around— including the dumb little tattletale boy from the first day that I got here.

"Come in, sit down." The mean Uncle growls, after he opens the door to let me in. His deep brown eyes bore into the skin on my feet and I shift my weight uncomfortably. "Yo' moddah dem left me one note fo' say you was coming fo' hang wit' us 'til Sunday ah?"

I nod.

"She must t'ink I running some kind of halfway house or somet'ing'."

I consider leaving, but the air smells really good in here; like freshly baked pizza or warm, sweet bread. My stomach makes no secret that it desires something to eat. It roars so loud I'm reminded of the ocean again. I want to eat, and I want to run. Maybe I'll do both. I'll eat, and then run. Or I'll run while I eat. If I can just make my way into the kitchen…

"Boy, what I said? Come sit down."

Where? Where do I sit? There are little kids everywhere. Kids jumping on the couch, kids wrestling on the floor, kids along the walls, some standing in corners. But I walk further into the house and find a place to sit. All I can find is a stool.

Uncle goes into the kitchen and I'm stuck watching the little trolls. I count them. One and two boys kicking each other in the face and stomach on the ground, two little girls jumping on the couch, a boy bulldozing a book into a baby who is drawing on the wall, a boy and a girl in corners on the opposite side of the room. And the kid who would testify in a court of law that I was an evil bird terrorist, thumbing through a book about you guessed it: terrorists. No, I'm kidding. It's a book about birds.

That kid looks up and glares at me. "What are you doing here?"

"Sitting." I answer, as curt as I can. It's none of his business who, what, or why. My parents suck. They left me behind and now I have no choice but to stay here with you rotten people and that horrible, stupid man that I have to call Uncle.

"I can see that." He scoffs, like a rude little weasel. "I mean why are you here?"

Pssh. Like I'm telling you anything about me and my life. "Why are you here?" I ask.

"I live here." He answers, hands folded across his chest like a miniature Uncle Nalu.

I shrug like I don't care because I don't and look away. The boy is watching at me like I'm a criminal. It's making my skin crawl. "What?" I ask and puff out my chest the same way Joe-Joe did when he got all up in my face at the beach. The boy's eyes are fixed on me and I see a little bit of myself in the kid. I don't like it; it makes me feel sorry for him. So sorry that I'm about to throw the little guy some pocket-sized pity.

Too late. Uncle Nalu is back in the room. "Ready fo' eat?"

He's got pizza. I knew I smelled a pizza pie-uh. All the kids— myself included— start jumping up and down like frantic cult followers. Uncle laughs and places the pizza down on the table, then tells me and the tattletale boy to start passing the food out while he gets the other pizzas and our drinks.

The kid peels off the slices, and I hand them out. We both pick at the melted mozzarella that is begging to be eaten off of the pan, and watch Uncle Nalu disappear and then reappear with another one. He puts that one down, hands out a whole bunch of sippy cups with lids and pours vitamin D milk into each of them.

"I don't drink milk." I grumble, looking towards the kitchen for soda. And I don't drink out of sippy cups.

"Brah. I look like I care?" He snaps. He reaches over to his cup stack, pushes a cup into my hand and pours until the milk is all the way to the top. He pushes one of the lids with the sucker part on it and smirks. "Drink up, small boy." He says.

I hold the cup to my mouth, hold my breath and suck on it. It's thick and makes me want to barf and for some reason that seems to make Uncle happy. He smiles even bigger when I go to grab a piece of pizza and a little kid pushes me aside and takes the one I had my eyes on. I want to growl and snarl and snap but I:

KEEP CALM AND LET IT GO

I go over another kid's head and snatch up three fat pieces. Pile them up on my plate in a glorious pizza sandwich stack, and move back to my stool.

Uncle is chewing on his food with his mouth open, and telling everyone else to sit down, to be quiet, to eat nicely but no one is listening. No wonder he looks so stressed out and angry all the time. I sit there and think. Makena used to do this thing when I was a distracted kid with energy that wanted to go all over the place. What was it again? Oh yeah, I remember.

I get up, put my plate and cup down on my stool and pull out the dining chairs so the kids can sit down. "Simon says sit."

The kids all scamper and scuttle, giggling as they find a chair.

"Eat like a pig." I command.

Two of the littler ones— a boy and a girl— start to snort, but I shake my head and mimic Uncle Stuart's stupid cross face. Everyone else is holding back their laughter.

"Eat like a cow." I tell them.

The same two little ones make moo-ing noises. I lower my eyebrows at them and whip my head back from side to side.

"Simon says," I say, as slow as I can, "eat like Uncle Nalu."

They all laugh and mimic his eating habits. They chew with their mouths gaping wide, wipe their hands on their shirts and pants, shove as much pizza as they can into their faces. When he sees this, he stops, grabs and napkin, tucks it into the front of his shirt like a bib and starts eating like he thinks he's proper.

The little kids laugh and start acting like humans. Uncle Nalu raises his eyebrows, at me, and surprisingly mouths the words thank you. The kids all copy him. I sit back and eat until all the food is gone.

　　　⪼　✦　⪻

　　　After the dishes and all the kids are washed, Uncle Nalu tells me that he wants to talk to me. I roll my eyes and drag his feet as I walk behind him because I'm tired of being stuck here on this dumb island and just want my day to end. He flips the light switch that shines on the front porch and opens the door.

"Mahalo, Braddah. You alright."

I yawn, hoping it will signal to him how much I think about his little 'talk.'

It doesn't.

He leads me to the pair of wicker chairs outside and shuts the door behind us. "No, I mean it. You helped me a lot tonight. Appreciate it."

I nod. Yawn again. This time, out of actual exhaustion.

Uncle Nalu is studying me, my face, my seated position— which is all the way at the edge of the seat, bent forward with my elbows on both knees and my chin in my palms. I wonder if he knows how uncomfortable I am around him. Wonder if he knows how mean I think he is.

"You t'ink I mean, yeah?"

I sit up straight. Great. Another person who can probably read my mind. I shrug even though the whole of me is invested in seeing him as a being of pure evil.

He chuckles to himself, sits back and folds his arms back so that the back of his head is resting in his folded hands. He throws his right ankle onto his left knee and gazes at the termites fluttering in the light. "Look. I sorry I been so hard on you boy. I just, I no like…"

My Dad. My Mom. Me. That we came here and booted you out of your house. My dead sister. Our disturbance of your life. All of the above.

"Maybe now is not da time for tell…" He mutters instead of giving me a straight answer.

You can't do that to me, you can't just tell me something and decide you're not going to tell me anymore!

"Stress, I tell you." Uncle Nalu sighs. He picks a termite off of his calf and pops it's guts out between his thumb and index finger. "I— I sorry I read yo' lettah from da haole girl." Uncle Nalu is trying to connect with me and I don't know why but it's making me uncomfortable. I think we're better off when we're both hating on each other.

"S'awight." I answer, trying to play it cool but inside, it really stings that he would do that— embarrass me for the third time in front of a really hott girl. In the same day.

"Naw I mean it. I seen you spocking out da kine. So since you help me, I going help you and try hook you up wit' Napua." He sits back and smiles so big my eyes squint from the shine coming off of his teeth.

My breaking heart beats faster and I swear it's going to bust open like a piñata at any moment. "Naw, no thanks Uncle Cree…Uncle Nalu." The words spurt out of my mouth like soda from a shaken can. What are you saying? No! She may be really weird and irritating but she is hott. And if Deanna doesn't want me…

"Nah, you one good kid. I going." He takes a deep breath and looks back at his front door. "You see da kids in mah house?"

I nod again. Yawn. How could I not see them? They're everywhere.

"They good kids too, you know."

I roll my eyes upwards and pretend I'm watching the light. Yeah, good kids. That's why they were wrecking everything and beating each other up so much.

"They are." He repeats like some kind of greasy car salesman trying to butter up the buyer. "That's the future of paddling, right dea. All of dem dey all coming wit' us tomorrow."

"What's tomorrow?" I yawn.

"Your parents nevah tell you?"

I shrug. Wait— maybe this is what they wanted to talk to me about so badly. "No." I finally answer.

"Ho, dey no tell you nuttin.' We going camping."

"Ugh." I moan. It comes out a lot louder than I expect. "I meant that as a compliment."

"Yeah, right." Uncle Nalu frowns. "No worry, you going learn how fo' fit in yet."

EIGHTEEN

Not sure if it was the pizza, or my parents, or Uncle Nalu's couch but I had the weirdest dream. Makena's face appeared just as I was drifting off to nightmare land. If it were any other day, I would have freaked but I was too tired and nothing was going to keep me from diving into the blackness that surrounded me.

I followed her beckoning hands. She took me to a beach that looked almost like the one I paddled at today— one with a short band of tan sand separating water from grass. We stood there for a while, silent, watching the waves fall over the glassy surface, watching layers of white foam appear and dissolve along the tops of the bumps that brought the ocean to our feet. Beneath our toes, smooth glass and polished shells glimmered and she smiled at the sight of it. It made me feel bad that I got to swim it and she didn't so I turned and walked away. She grabbed my shoulder and pointed at a dolphin leaping in the air.

"I thought you had something to do with that." I remember saying. "I wish you let me drown."

Her entire face frowned— eyebrows turned themselves downward towards the bridge of her nose, and her harsh eyes shrunk and seemed to scold me. She shook her head at me and grabbed my wrist. We went to an empty black room where the ugly jar sat on a tall, marble pedestal. She traced her fingers along the cheap vessel and shook her head. Her eyes narrowed and she shot me a look that clearly read, 'I hate this thing.'

I could see the remnants of the designs I made, the artfully written letters that I added to try and give Kena a better place; stuff that Mom and Dad ripped off in an attempt to keep the plastic pristine. It made sense. They took her jar away with them so I wouldn't hurt it again. And they took themselves away so I wouldn't hurt them…

"I hate it too." I muttered. I wanted to rip it off the pedestal and throw it across the room but instead, I laid into Makena. "Why'd you leave me alone, huh? Mom is crazy nuts and Dad looks like he's formulating his escape plan. I caught him outside flirting with one of Mom's sisters. Can you believe that? And she was flirting back! These people are such dicks and the man I'm staying with right now is a perpetual douchebag. I can't do anything right; everyone here thinks I'm such a screw up. I hate it here. I hate my life. I can't live like this. I can't. I—" At this point, I started to cry in my dreams but not in real life because like Dad says, real men can't cry because real men don't get tears, "I don't have anyone, Kena. Mom and Dad don't want me. Not even Deanna wants me. I just want to be where you are."

She grabbed my hulking biceps *hey I said it was a dream* and shook me hard. "*Oh shut up, crybaby wiener. At least you're alive. At least you can say that you've been in the water, in a canoe, in the back of a pickup truck. At least you can say that you've hugged grandma, that you've spent time with grandpa, that you're still able to talk to mom and dad. You can say that you've met our relatives. You can learn our culture. You have a home. You have no idea how big that is, how much that means to me. I wish I could be in your place. I would accept it— all of it and all of them with an open heart. Open your eyes, buttface, wake up. You control your life. So what if you have a few hard times, so what if it's taking you a while to try to fit in. Stop trying to make everyone fold to whatever shape you're accustomed to. Stop expecting them to convert to your deluded and warped sense of perfection because perfection does not exist. Stop trying to turn yourself into a martyr because I don't feel sorry for you."*

I hated her. Not because she was making things up, or because I thought she was trying to be mean, I hated her because she was right.

"And another thing," she added before I had the chance to say anything more to her, *"you didn't kill me. Okay? So stop saying that. Go find my phone and read the last thing I wrote. I killed me. We're in charge of our own lives, buttface. We make our own choices. No one owes you anything, Gabriel. No one."*

And just as fast as she came, she was gone. Everything was black again.

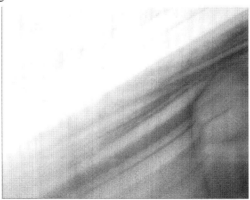

NINETEEN

I wake up to two smiling girls at the foot of Uncle Nalu's couch. U'i and Mirry. Ugh. I roll over, expecting to be left alone, when one of them shoves an unpeeled banana into my face. I want to reach out and slap someone but they're dumb girls and I'm not supposed to hit 'em no matter how stupid they are so I roll over until I'm balled up face-down.

They climb on my back and proceed to ride me like a horse while cheering that we are going to plant and harvest taro today. "Get out of here." I mumble and play dead. They go away for a long time, but after a while, heavy footsteps enter my Uncle's living room and a skinny body sits on my tailbone. "Get off!" I roar and buck until whoever it is falls off.

"Ow!" A girl yells. Good for you. You deserved it. "Fine," she says, "be like that. I was going to ask you if you wanted to sit by me today but I'll just sit by one of your cousins instead."

I look up so I can see whose face the voice belongs to. Napua. "Sorry." I say, and push my hair back so I look somewhat human. "I thought you were…"

"Yeah. I know." She says, and flicks her salon commercial quality hair back. At least she's smiling at me. Napua is in an

oversized t-shirt and long denim shorts that look like they belong
to her grandmother boo. At least her face looks kind of pretty.
"Come on, get up, get ready. Everyone's asking where you are.
We're leaving in a few minutes."

I groan, roll off the couch and head back to my house to
grab some clothes.

No one's home and it weirds me out. Usually, I can count
on my parents being there but everything is quiet, and closed up
tight. When my sister was alive, even if she wasn't talking to me
I'd feel better knowing she was somewhere in the house, but now,
it's so crypt-like, I'm scared I'll walk into her ghost.

I know I can make all the noise I want because no one can
hear me, and no one would complain, but I'm not even tempted
to. I don't know what I'll disturb if I let it be known that I am
there, so I sneak around, packing Dad's old fart bag with my
stuff. I do the sniff test on everything and notice none of what
I have has been washed for at least a month now; but I figure
everyone else looks like a hobo so it's okay if I smell like one.
Blanket, pillow, socks, towel, shirt, shorts. I'm going to be bored
out of my gourd. Someone's honking a car horn outside. I don't
even have time to brush my teeth. I scurry into my sister's room,
try to remember where I kicked her little box with the notes in it,
can't find anything, shoot into the living room and grab a random
book off of the bookshelf and throw it in my bag.

Someone's knocking.

"Gabe, we're going." Ugh. Uʻi just opened the door

without an invitation.

And double ugh. Mirry is right behind her. "Yeah, Uncle's leaving you behind if you don't get out now."

"I'm coming, I'm coming." I grumble, and shut the door behind me and my stupid cousins.

TWENTY

I'm in the bed of Uncle Nalu's pickup truck reading about the overthrow of Queen Lili'uokalani in her book, "*Hawai'i's Story by Hawai'i's Queen*" when we pull into a dirt road. The words on the pages are jumping up and down as I struggle to read them, but I can't keep them still enough to make out what they say. I sigh, put the book back in Dad's fart bag and zip it up.

I think for a bit about what she went through, how she became Hawaii's Queen and was charged and later arrested for trying to write a constitution on behalf of her people, and how some of the naturalized foreigners objected to it. It didn't make sense. I didn't know peasants had the right to do that—just arrest a Queen for ruling her own government. Wasn't that her job? I wonder if anyone would arrest Queen Elizabeth for trying to make a law today. Probably not. It's so unfair. No wonder my cousins don't like mainlanders.

The truck pulls off to the side of the road and everyone is getting out of Grandpa's SUV, Aunty Jo's car, and Aunty Vai's minivan. Uncle Nalu parks the car and the little kids hop out of it and stretch. I leave my bag and follow everyone else to where the grass parts. Grandpa leads us up a short path and we stop at a clearing. I peer behind him and everybody else and see the most beautiful garden I've ever seen. Not beautiful as in flowers and enchanted fairies beautiful, or even vegetables lined up in rows beautiful but beautiful in an unspoiled and different kind of way. Here, there are several rectangular 'ponds' filled with water, and green plants with huge leaves that are shaped like hearts. Banks that serve as land bridges that are wide enough for two people to walk across are alongside each one, and there are all kinds of fruit trees and moving water everywhere.

"Kū" Grandpa sings, long and low, and right away everyone but me starts chanting:

"Kūnihi ka mauna i ka la'i ē
'O Wai'ale'ale lā i Wailua
Huki a'ela i ka lani

Ka papa auwai o Kawaikini
Alai ʻia aʻela e Nounou, nalo Kaipuhaʻa
Ka laulā ma uka o Kapaʻa ē
Mai paʻa i ka leo
He ʻole ka hea mai ē"

A woman's voice replies:

"Aloha na hale o makou i maka-maka ole,
Ke alanui hele mauka o Puʻu-kahea la, e-e!
Ka-he-a!
E Kahea aku ka pono e komo mai oe iloko nei.
Eia ka puʻu nui o waho nei, he anu"

Grandpa moves forward again and we all follow behind him like a row of ducks. The woman laughs and walks up to Grandma. She's a middle-aged woman with Asian features, and long brown hair that hits her waist. They touch foreheads, and hug, and then she and Grandpa do the same.

I watch her scary smile *she looks familiar* as she appraises all of us *where have I seen her before?* She draws her attention to Uʻi and Mirry *was it from the beach? No* and rests on Aunty Jo *maybe from the shave ice line a couple of weeks ago?* They hug and her gaze moves on *where have I seen that face?* She stops again at Aunty Vai, who coldly pats her on the back, and then smiles at me. *Oh God, now I remember! She's the woman that threw Makena away—the one from the plane, what was her name? I think it was Donna Harper.* I think she recognizes me too because her face turns white, and then bright red.

175

"Mom, are you okay?" Napua asks and runs over to hug the woman. *Mom? Ugh I should have known, Napua Harper, Donna Harper. But what are the chances, what are the odds?*

She lowers her eyes and smiles at her muddied toes. "No I'm fine hon. Come on, let's get you guys in the loʻi."

She starts to walk away but she's not going to get away that easily. I know Makena wouldn't have wanted it that way. I take a few strides in her direction and stick out my hand. "Hi. I'm Gabe."

Her lip is quivering and she holds out her hand. *She's pretending she doesn't even know me*. "Nice to meet you, Gabe."

"Do you work on the airplane?" I ask, hoping she'll bite. She shakes her head.

"What? Mom." Napua smiles at me, and takes my hand. "She does. She's a flight attendant."

"I thought I recognized you." I say, and she looks up at me with eyes that scream, 'please don't tell on me' something about those eyes stops me, and I shrug. "I think you were on the flight the day me and my parents came." Is all I say. She looks at me as if to say, 'thank you for not saying more,' but I'm not trying to be her friend. I give her the old two fingers tracing the invisible trail from my eyes to her signal and don't take my eyes off of her until she looks away first.

"Say what?" Napua squeaks, completely oblivious to what's been going on. "That is so cool." Still holding my hand, she leads me to the edge of a mud pond. "You know, Mom sees all kinds of people on her flights. One time she said she even saw the guy, you know, the guy from the news, the one with the wavy white toupee who always says, 'ain't life great?' After every emotional story?"

I don't know who she's talking about or why she's holding on to my hand but I don't want her to stop touching me so I say, "yeah, that guy's cool."

"Ew, what?" She says. "No he's not, he's a total goob."

"That's what I said." I'm backtracking. "I said, that guy's a goob."

"No you didn't."

"Yes I did." I feel her hand releasing from mine.

"You are such a liar." It's gone. She took it back. She's at the waterline now, daintily touching her toenail in the pool, I'm guessing to test the temperature. I want to push her in for calling me a liar, but I manage to control myself. She dips her foot in down to her ankle, and I follow behind her. I blink, and she grabs me by the wrist and yanks me as hard as she can. I slip and try to grab on to her but she ducks and I flip over her back and fall into the mud. "Oops." She says, covering her mouth.

"You did that on purpose," I yelp. The water is freezing and the mud is even colder under my heels.

"No I didn't." She's trying to play innocent.

"Liar!" I yell, and grab her by her wrists.

"You better not— Gabe, you better…" too late, I pull her wrists lightly and she falls chest first into the mud. "You're so stupid!" She squeaks and starts throwing fistfuls of poop smelling mud at me. I do the same, and grab handfuls of vile mud to drop on her head. I'm about to dump it on her when I feel something moving in my hands. I don't know what I'm expecting—maybe a bug, or an earthworm or something like that—but what I'm holding is a fat brown toad. I throw it at her—not on purpose, but out of reflex and she starts shrieking.

The adults come running. "What the—what are you kids doing? Get out of there right now!" Grandma bellows. "You folks stop playing around. Get out of that lo'i and come help us pick kalo. Right now, before I make you loloheads plant dis whole place."

I shake the mud off of my hands as we make our way out of the lo'i, and use my thumb and pointer finger to squeeze the excess from my palms to my fingertips. It has the consistency of brownie mix and it's dripping off my face and onto my lips. Napua grins at me and I'm almost tempted to stick my tongue out and taste the smelly clay when I look down. There are hundreds of baby frogs—not tadpoles because these ones have little feet and hands—under my toes. Some of those feet and arms are detached from little frog bodies. I want to throw up.

Napua crinkles her nose at me. "You're such a wuss." There. Finally. Someone says what I know everyone around me has been thinking all along.

"I'm a frog killer. I just killed these baby frogs." I babble.

"Oh please. You didn't just kill those frogs." She takes on a tone that I assume a sociopath would use. "You also killed shrimp, and mosquitos, and earthworms, and crayfish, and fish…"

First I killed my sister by texting her, and now I have all of this extra guilt. "I'm sorry."

"Oh shut up." She sasses and offers me her hand as a way out of the square pond. "My Dad says, 'where there is death, there is life.'" I feel like she's going to push me back in if I take her hand, but I take it anyway. I figure if she tries to push me, I'll pull her back in. She doesn't. Instead, she pulls with all she has in her until I'm out of there. "What you think is bad actually has a purpose. Those dead things in there? That's just the circle of life. You see it all now because it's right there in front of you; but sooner or later, it won't be as fresh— but it will always be there."

She's so poetic. "In our minds and in our hearts?" I interrupt.

"What?" She's laughing at me now. "No, psycho. In the pond. As fertilizer. Ugh. The point I'm trying to make is that those dead things right there, they're not just dead things floating around everywhere, they help with the growth. Sure it'll stink around here for a while, but eventually, the smell of it will go away, and their imprints will stay right here, giving whatever they have to the plants. And the plants will drain what they can from them and continue to grow. I guess what I'm trying to say is, it's how we take care of what is living that is really important. Life will keep living and dead things will keep dying for like, ever— and there's nothing you can do about it so just get over it."

While 'Confucius' over there is standing around preaching at me to 'just get over it', the space in my family that my sister held is forever gone because in case she may have forgotten, my sister is dead, but Aunty Vai is at us now. "You two—get ovah dea right now!"

"Yes, Aunty." Napua moans and elbows me. It makes me smile beneath my drying mud mask, and we slosh towards the family.

TWENTY ONE

The whole taro plant is sacred to Hawaiian people, according to Grandma. "Long time ago, Wakea the sky father and Hoʻo-ho-ku-ka-la-ni the wreath of stars in the heavens had a stillborn child who they called Ha-loa-na-ka-lau-ka-pa-li-li. With grief, they buried their eldest child and one day they found that a heart shaped plant started to grow from the soil that they put him in. Kalo." She explained, and lifted one out of the loʻi. "Soon after, Hoʻo-ho-ku-ka-la-ni became pregnant again and had a living child who was called, 'Haloa.' He is the descendant of Hawaiian nobility; those who took care of their people. To us Hawaiians, this plant here, this kalo is like a brother. He looks after us, and we look after him."

From Grandpa I learned that kalo is the corm of the plant, and that the corm is the big bulbous potato looking thing that grows at the bottom. The huluhulu are the roots that grow out of the underbelly of the corm, and the ʻoha is the little bud that comes out of the top. I also learned that the ha is the stem, that the kohina is the top of the taro, the replantable part is called the huli, that luau is the leaf, and that it has little spikes on it

180

that makes you itchy. That was the part that everyone harvested barebacked in the morning sun.

I also learned that the water that comes out from a sun-cooked water hose after a few long half-naked hours in cold water does not feel as good as it sounds like it does—especially after getting a sunburn that stings like a mofo, and that the rancid smell of the mud does not leave your hands no matter what you scrub with and no matter how many times you scrub. But it *does* make my skin feel softer than a baby's foot. (Hey, I've never been gross enough to touch a baby's butt so sue me.)

I've already helped my grandparents wash the luʻau leaves, and assemble this food they call laulau by stacking seven leaves, and putting a piece of pork, a piece of butterfish, and a pinch of salt in the center, and then wrapping it up so that it looks like a ball. Grandma and my Aunties finished it off by placing it in the middle of two leaves from a plant that they called, 'ti' and tying it together. Grandpa stacked it in the steamer and let it go, while Uncle Nalu worked on cooking other things with Napua's mom.

Right now everyone is sitting around under a big wooden shelter with a thatched grass roof, waiting for food to cook and things to happen. The little kids that live with Uncle Nalu are playing chase, the slightly older ones are lying around trying to figure out how to 'destroy' ants by dumping carbonated sugar all over their anthills, (I told you they weren't smart) and my cousins and Grandparents are bringing their instruments out from their cars to play music.

"Hoo-tah!" Uʻi says, grabbing an old ukulele from Joe-Joe's hand. "Au-ryte. Kanikapila, baby!" Her eyes meet mine and she smiles hard so that her dimples cave in. "That means play music for fun and whatevers."

I shrug and watch all my cousins take hold of something. Mirry has a long wooden tube made out of bamboo with holes in it. She calls it a nose flute and blows into it with one nostril while sealing the other one shut with her thumb. Napua leans in and tells me that 'ohe hano ihu' is the correct name for it. Joe-Joe's got a bigger ukulele, and George has some kind of a brown gourd that looks like a squash but sounds like a drum. "Ipu." Napua informs me, while I nod. Grandma's got her guitar, and me, there are no instruments left for *me not that I know how to play anything anyway*, so I'm stuck playing the world's tiniest violin.

Everyone is singing and clapping, and playing, and having a really good time and I'm just watching and trying to see where I can fit in. I don't see how I can so I get up, and kick rocks. Times like these are when I really miss Makena. And yeah, I mean, miss her miss her. Bad teeth, rancid breath and all because at least it meant that I wasn't alone in life. Now she's, well she's like Haloa's older brother only her being dead isn't providing me with anything but grief.

"Gabe!" Napua's voice is coming from my right side, so I wipe my eyes and spin around.

"What's up?" I ask, waiting for her to give me some more advice on how to act, or what to believe or whatever. She doesn't say anything, just walks with me. We walk for a long time, not saying a syllable, and the whole time, I'm just trying to figure out what to say.

"You like it here?" She finally asks.

No. I don't. I don't fit in. I don't know where I belong.

Sister's in a jar. Mom and Dad are never around. I don't feel like I have a family anymore. "Yeah." I answer, and shrug.

"Liar." She giggles.

"Not lying." I say. "And by the way, thanks for the speech about the dead things earlier. Made me feel a lot better."

She slaps my arm this time. "You are such a liar!"

"Ow," I pull back playfully. "What makes you think I'm lying?"

"Because I know."

"How do you know?" I want to know, so I can find a better way to conceal my realness from her.

"Because I know, okay?" Napua sighs in a way that says get over it, don't ask me about that again.

I shrug, and we walk some more. I can't think of anything more to say so I concentrate on the sounds our shoes make as they walk along the path. The crunching, the rock popping, the stumble every now and then when one of us kicks a root that tries to knock us down. I listen to the tinkle of the running water as it bubbles over stones and into the taro ponds. I hear the gossip of the birds, the faint roar of car tires on paved road, smell the mud between my fingernails, and my upper lip.

"You're quiet." She says, softly. And then, "You have anything you want to talk about?"

Like what?

"Anything you want to unload? Go on, if you do, you can just tell it to me. I know what you're going through, I understand."

She lost a sister too? "Naw."

"Liar." She growls. "I really wish you'd stop doing that to

183

me."

"Stop what?" I ask, even though I know perfectly well what she's talking about.

"Lying." She says. "I want you to tell me what you're going through. I want to know more about you." More silence. Then, "do you miss her?"

I wonder if she's growing impatient with me. I don't want her to leave, so I say what I really feel for once. "Hell yeah, I miss her. I miss her every day."

"Oh." She says, and bites into her bottom lip.

"I never told her I loved her, never told her I cared, never even realized how important she was in my life until she was gone. And you know what the worst part is?"
It felt good coming out, and I was feeling braver by the second. "I killed her."

"You what?" She asked, her eyes growing larger.

"I killed her." There. I said it again. Cuff me and throw me in prison now.

She looks confused. "Your girlfriend?"

"Wait—what?" I had no idea what she was asking me. "I don't have a girlfriend—I'm—I'm talking about Makena. My sister."

"Ohh…" Napua sighs and stops walking. "I was asking if—if you missed—I mean, that's the part that I meant when I said I knew… never mind. You miss your *sister*. But how, I mean what do you mean you *killed* her, I heard she died in a car accident."

I stop and sit down right in the middle of the trail. "She did." *Now I'm in trouble. I said too much and now I have to explain my way out of it.* "They said she died while texting and... I think she might have been texting me because I was texting her that day. I never told anyone, not my Mom or my Dad and I even got rid of the proof by throwing my phone away after it happened so you have to promise not to say a word, not even to U'i and especially not to Mirry..."

Napua nods and crosses her heart with her index finger.

"The night she died Makena said some things and I was so mad I went blind with rage so when she left, I wrote her all kinds of stupid things. I told her I wanted her to die, that she deserved it but I mean, I didn't want to kill her, it just—it—I didn't want to but I did."

"Gabe," Napua plops herself in my lap as if I'm some kind of string-bean bag chair. "People say all kinds of things when we're mad. That doesn't mean you killed her."

It doesn't? "But I wished it on her. I told her I wished she would die. I remember specifically saying that. Over and over again."

"I say it to people all the time," Napua whispers into my ear like it's some kind of secret. "It's never happened, but that doesn't mean that I actually wish it would just like I don't believe you actually wished she'd die." She nuzzles her head into the side of my head and hugs me hard. "Sometimes, things are just coincidences. Sometimes things just happen. When they're good they're called a blessing and when they're bad,"

"They're curses." I finish.

"Accidents." She corrects me. "They're called accidents. No one's fault but hers."

I push her off of me. It can't be true. Makena was

innocent. It's my fault she's dead. I'm off and running.

"She shouldn't have been on her phone. Everyone makes mistakes, Gabe. That's the beauty of life. *The lessons.* You know, you can't go through your life wishing you did something different, you can't change things once they happen. You have to learn from the bad stuff. Stop running! You can't run forever" She calls after me, "Gabe, come back; nobody's perfect."

TWENTY TWO

The partying goes on all night but it doesn't matter; I'm zipped up in my tent reading Queen Liliʻuokalani's book from the beginning this time. I'm halfway through when someone unzips the door of my tent.

"Oh, sorry." It's Napua. "I didn't know you were in here."

"Liar." I sigh.

"For serious." She says.

I shake my head. I don't know what Uncle Nalu told her about me, but the girl won't leave me alone. She's worse than Uʻi. But I figure, might as well let her in because she looks cold, so I say, "come."

"Can't." She says. "My Mom and Dad will have a pissy fit if they find out I'm even talking to you this late at night."

Did she just say pissy fit? Lols. That's not even right. I shrug and go back to reading my book. "No worries. I guess I'll see you later than."

She doesn't leave. Instead she's asking, "is that Hawaiʻi's Story?"

I nod.

"I love that book." She continues, and opens the door all the way to let herself in. I make room for her and she lies down next to me. I can feel her reading over my shoulder, so I move my book so she can see it better. The two of us read together in silence for what feels like hours. "Unreal, yeah?" She says when we get to the end, where the story turns into genealogy pages.

I nod. "No wonder my cousins hate mainland people."

"They don't *hate* they distrust." She says, but she can't convince me. I distrust my parents but I still treat them good. Hate is when you just don't like someone for no real or rational reason. Hate is how they feel about me.

"Sure." I say, "no they hate me, and they *really* hate my father."

"Well that…" she mutters, "I've heard stories and well, there's a lot more to that than you think there is."

"What do you mean?" I wonder out loud, my memory taking me back to Aunty Vai's slap and us moving away in the first place.

"Ew." Napua says instead of giving me an answer, but I follow her finger to the ceiling of the tent. There are little termites—and I know they're termites because they kept falling in our food tonight and everyone was calling them that—all over the walls, the door, everywhere. "Ugh," she whines, "close the doors and the windows before the whole colony winds up in here. Puh-lease."

I do, and we lay back down. We're both quiet for a long time. I'm cutting ugly bugs that wiggle out from their wings in half with my stinkernails, and right when I think of something good to say, right when I'm going to tell her that I think I like her way more than I liked Deanna, I turn my head to Napua but she's sleeping. I'm exhausted, and I don't want to wake her because I'm tired of being alone and it's nice to have someone to talk to, so I throw the blanket on her and let myself shiver.

>　❋　<

I wake up to beams of flashlights in my face, and a man's voice yelling at Napua. "What are you doing in dea, girl? Who you sleeping with?"

Napua jolts up and covers her face with her arm. "Daddy! I'm not—we weren't—we weren't doing anything."

The man reaches in and grabs his daughter out by the arm, and then climbs in the tent with me. "You touch my daughter." His light is in my face.

"Daddy, no, he didn't do anything to me. We were talking story and I fell asleep, that's all I promise. We just fell asleep."

"You mess wit' my daughter— eh, if I find out you knocked her up bulleh, I going knock you…" He growls, without moving his flashlight out of my eyes.

I'm so nervous I could pee. Or barf. Or both. I don't know what to say; I've never been confronted by so many grown-up men before in my life so I answer, "duh-duh-buh-uh-duh." *Yeah, I really told him. Put that in the bank and sit on it, dude.*

"Dad. What you doing?" Great, sounds like another man is bent on making his way into my tent.

"Dis punk was sleeping wit' Napua."

A face peers in at me but I can't make it out. All I can see is the outline of long, bushy hair and some wide shoulders.

reminds me a little of Uncle Nalu. "Him? Nah. He still one little kid."

"An' so what? Kids not always kids, I know dat fo' sure."

"Nah, dis one's innocent." The voice says again, more soothing this time.

"How you know, ah?" The faceless man snaps.

The other man lowers his voice a little. "Dass da kine dem's son. You know, hopeless and hapless."

"For real?" The guy who's in my face finally puts his flashlight down. "What your name?"

My eyes are still adjusting to the world. "Gabe."

"Gabe?" The man's voice booms, and bam. I feel a large, sandpapery hand clap me on my sunburn. "You was da boy flailing around at da beach da oddah day?"

It hurts. "Um yeah."

"You know him, Dad?" The other man's voice says from outside. I swear it sounds like Uncle Nalu but there's no way.

My eyes are seeing more than shadows now. They see shapes and colors. I study the face in front of me. "You remembah me, oh what?"

I immediately recognize that face. "Ikaika?"

"Brah!" He's shouting, and suddenly he's happy—too happy. "Your Mom is Haunani?"

"Marcel." I answer. It feels less likely that I am going to die.

"Mar—who?"

"His Mom's Haunani. She changed her name, membah? She nevah like be found."

The guy outside says. I can only make out his surf shorts,

190

his hairy legs and his mangled looking feet.

"Dass right. Dass right. You have one sistah too uh? Where she stay?"

I shake my head. "Not anymore."

"What you mean, not anymore?" He growls, suddenly on the verge of attacking me once again.

"She…" *I'm so tired of explaining this to everyone. I don't have a sister anymore and the more I keep saying it the more it hurts. Please don't—don't make me say it again.*

The guy standing outside drops down to his knees, and motions to Ikaika to move towards him. *It is Uncle Nalu.* He whispers something in his ear while I cry into my folded knees and arms like a stupid, wussy little baby.

"Damnit!" Ikaika shouts and pounds his fists into the ground. I look up, and he leans over to hug me. "Sorry, son. I sorry. Nobody told me." I sob when I hear the word son—I haven't felt like anyone's son for a long, long time.

"Kay den Dad. I going check on da imu den." Uncle Nalu says, and pops Ikaika in the shoulder.

"Why— does— he-keep—keep— call-i-hing— y-y-you Da—ha—dad?" I ask between sniffles. Ugh. I can't even speak English.

Ikaika doesn't loosen his grip when he says, "Because I am. His Dad."

I try to push him away because, there's no way— Grandpa is his father.

"We had him when we were young." Ikaika says.

"We?" I ask. *At least I could formulate one English word.*

"Takes mo den one person for get one bebe," he laughs,

and finally lets me go. "We was supposed to get married—we knew each oddah long time, since we was kids, an' den she met one haole guy who talked her into getting wit' him instead."

And like that, all crying subsides. It's like he turned off the switch. I'm one hundred percent fine. On the outside.

"Had races, yeah? So we went for stay at dis hotel in Waikiki," *Oh God I know this story,* "and he was all ga-ga ovah her," *this is Dad's story,* "which nevah matter to me, I mean, she was beautiful, okay? Planny guys admire beauty," *SHE is MOM* "and dats okay because cannot help if you born wit' good looks; but dis guy, he was one snake. He fool around wit' da sistahs— fool around wit' Vai first, den Jo, an' den finally, after we had baby girl, they up an' left. Took the bebe and ran away, left Nalu boy wit' da parents an' ran. Was his idea, I guess. She not dumb li' dat. At least I keep telling myself dat."

If Makena was born before she went to California, who's her father? Who's my father? Who's U'i's father? No wonder Uncle Nalu hates me. No wonder Grandpa calls him, 'your braddah.' What is wrong with my family?

I feel brave. "You're Nalu *and* Makena's dad?"

He nods. Oh God.

"Nalu is my brother?" *Again: no wonder Uncle Nalu hates me.* "Are you *my* Dad too?"

He shakes his head no. At least there's that.

"And U'i…"

Ikaika squirms a little. "No."

Thank God. He tilts his head to the left and right, stretching his thick neck, and blurts, "Not mine. She's your Dad's."

192

Ugh. No wonder she said she was my sister. So what next? Is he going to tell me that Joe-Joe and Georgie are also my brothers? What's wrong with them? No wonder they ran away. Even I, knowing what I now know want to run away.

"Joe-Joe and George my Dad's too?"

Ikaika shakes his head emphatically. *Whew.*

"Sorry, ah braddah. I thought you knew."

And then, just like earlier, I feel like another switch is turned on with his words—but this one does not calm me down. I stand up inside the tent and start punching the walls.

"Ho easy brah. Easy." Ikaika says, and moves back a little to give me room.

"I hate everyone!" I scream, not caring that the voice coming out from inside of me makes me sound like I'm being possessed.

"Forgive, brah. Forgive."

I keep swinging until the tent drops down all over us. I can feel Ikaika escaping, can feel his thick hands wrap around my ankles, and with one hard yank, I'm out of there. It's early in the morning, I don't know where I'm going but I don't plan on stopping.

"No run, brah. Be one man. Stand firm. Forgive. No run."

I don't listen. I run until my sides hurt and then I run some more.

I don't know how, but I manage to find myself back at the beach that my Grandparents go paddling. There are a couple of homeless guys lying underneath the boats when I get there, but they don't look like they're doing anything so I don't bother with trying to chase them away. I don't know where else to go so I find a place under a tree and watch the sky turn brighter.

TWENTY THREE

They found me. I don't know how, but they found me. When I heard Uʻi and Napua scream my name my immediate instinct was to run towards them but I did the opposite and walked down to the water instead.

"Braddah." That voice *I know* is Ikaika's. "You bettah man up an' stop running away."

I don't know what else to do, I have nowhere else to go; I don't even know where my parents are at this point. So many lies. Too many lies. I see a big splash in the ocean. *Makena.* I go to it. *I'm coming Kena. Don't leave without me.*

"Poʻo paʻakiki, hard head" Ikaika is yelling, but I don't care. I keep going out to where I saw the dolphin—the naiʻa, I think it's called, the last time.

I'm in over my head and I'm trying not to panic. I can handle this, I got this, I can swim. I can swim. Breathe. Breathe. Scissor kick. Tread water. My head is bobbing above the top of the sea now, the water's so cold, so cold. I see a dorsal fin where the splash was— *it's the dolphin*— And I kick my way towards it.

I'm close enough now that I can touch it *ooh it's fast* and I reach my hand out.

"Boy! You stupid, or what?" Ikaika is shouting, but he sounds closer.

I turn away from the voices, I don't care anymore. I don't want to be here. Makena can take me. The dolphin is circling me, faster and faster. I splash so I can get it's attention.

There's a loud noise behind me and a whole bunch of men screaming. "Get out of there you stupid idiot!"

I finally turn and see Ikaika, Uncle *is he still Uncle?* Nalu, Joe-Joe, Georgie, and John, the boy I punched paddling towards me in a canoe. And they're making all kinds of noises. Great. Wonderful.

"Stop!" I sputter. "Stop! You're scaring away the nai'a!"

Uncle Nalu is the first to yell, "Dass not one nai'a you dummy, dass one manō!"

"What's a manō?" I ask. It's so close to me now I can touch it.

"Shark, stupid boy! Shark!" Ikaika screams, and suddenly, I feel panicked. My arms start flailing around and I'm kicking faster and faster and…

"Stop moving, you're attracting it!" John's low voice booms. *Oh so you want me to sink? Is that what you want?*

"Hurry up!" I call—oh God it rubbed me, it's skin touched my skin and it's rough.

"Punch 'em in da face!" Joe-Joe instructs, making fists of his own and swinging them left and right like a boxer.

Now is not the time for MMA. "I don't know how to punch in the water," I shout back. I am going to die so I might as well confess. "No one ever taught me how to hit properly."

"You hit Johnny one good one," Georgie yells, and then adds, "someone jump in and save him."

Yes, save me.

A chorus of "I ain't jumping in," and "no look at me," follows.

Napua's voice pops in my head. '*You know, you can't go through your life wishing you did something different, you can't change things once they happen.*'

So I fight. Not for her, not for my parents, not for Makena, not for the rest of my family or the guys in the boat, but for me. I fight for me. I fight because I don't want to regret not fighting. I can see it's face; it's black, oval eyes, it's jagged teeth aimed at me and I punch it as hard as I can. It shoots away from me, and swims towards the boat. The shadow it's casting makes the six-man canoe look like a dingy.

"Swim!" Ikaika yells, and they paddle closer to me. I'm finally up against the boat, my face smashed against the fiberglass side. *Somebody pull me up.*

"Go in on the other side," Georgie is screaming. *You've got to be kidding me!*

"Shut up," Joe-Joe is yelling, "he has to get in the boat." To me, he's howling "get in the boat!"

"No, we're going to huli if he gets in that way," Georgie bellows.

"Everybody lean!" John calls out and he grabs my two arms and pulls me up out of the water. I fall in the canoe like a lump of fish and lay in a fetal position. I am so tempted to suck my thumb.

"Damn fool kid." Ikaika mutters from the back of the boat

and spits in the water. "Get up, you okay. Wait, you okay?"

My heart is banging on my chest and my whole body is shaking with this weird kind of energy that makes my whole body feel electric and my head feel like laughing and crying and screaming but I'm alive so I nod.

"You okay." He reiterates and tells me to move back and take the seat in front of him. I do, scooting around my cousins and John so I don't have to get back in the water, and he hands me a paddle. "Guess you nevah like die that bad." He laughs.

"No." I say and shake my head. "I never."

Everyone's laughing and hitting me, now but my eyes are scanning the water for the manō; the shark.

'Uncle' Nalu sees this and says, "let's make like da birds and get da flock outta hea."

"In agreeance." Ikaika's voice booms. "Hoʻomau-kau-kau," he calls, "that means get ready." *That was for me.* "E kau-pe; that means reach." *Again, mine.* "Huki." Everyone pulls. Except me. "Kay, you seat five yeah?" He says, from behind me. I shrug. "No, I not asking, I telling. You seat five. Nalu is one, Georgie is two, Johnny is three, Joe-Joe is four. You five."

I nod, "okay, so you're six?"

"No." He snaps. *John is calling, hut— ho.* "I da steersman. Da captain. I talk, you shut up. Okay? Okay." I nod again and listen. "One, tree, an' five start on da left. Two an' four on da right you got that?" I nod. *hut— ho.* "So when he go hut, he's telling you almost your time to change ovah. Kay? Means you get one more stroke before you switch to da oddah side so when he call ho," *hut— ho*, "you switch to da oddah side. You get it?" I nod. I don't get it. "Next change you up. Get ready."

Uncle Nalu and John are both paddling on the right, so I hold my paddle so it's on the left side. *I forget how to do this already— all I remember is triangle and pull. Is that right?*

"Brah, your paddle is backwards. Fix 'em quick." Ikaika tells me in a quiet voice. Guess he doesn't want me to feel embarrassed.

I turn the paddle blade around and see a blank black backing. *Oh that's right, advertisement goes in front. Hand, scoop, yeah.* I'm ready for it, waiting like a kid trying to time their jump in while two other people are turning the rope. *Hut— ho.* I get my paddle in there and pull as hard as I can.

"Timing, timing." Ikaika grumbles, "watch the rhythm, feel the rhythm of the boat." I close my eyes and dip my paddle. "Better, better but no just dip your paddle. Put it all da way in until your bottom hand touches da water. Follow Joe-Joe's body. See how he twists his core? Good, good. Twist and pull. Triangle. Like that. Nice, good. Better."

Are we going back yet? Hut— ho. I notice Joe-Joe is positioned at the edge of his seat so I move to the edge of mine too. I can see his feet—one is under his seat, the other one stretched out in front *hut—ho.* And they switch when he switches so I do the same. Right foot forward when I'm paddling on the right side, left foot forward when I'm paddling on my left. Top hand parallel to bottom hand— yup; triangle. Then I look over Joe-Joe and watch John instead. He's on the same side as me so it's easier to follow. He leans forward and twists, then pulls until he's sitting up and does it again. I mimic his style. *I got this, this is easy.*

"No bobbing. Da canoe stay rocking. You gotta sit still."

Ikaika growls. "Good job up dea guys, we running, we running."

So how am I supposed to paddle? No one else is sitting still. I don't know what I'm doing. This is hard. Dad said it's fourteen on the right, fourteen on the left but I swear I counted more than that sometimes and less than that during other changes. I wonder if John knows how to count. *Aargh this is never ending. And where are we going, anyway?*

"Good, good boy, good." Ikaika tells me.

Woof.

We paddle forever and slow down when we see another outrigger sitting out by a buoy. "Dey need help, oh what?" Ikaika asks I-don't-know-who because everyone's eyes are on the paddle in front of them and nobody's eyes are really looking around. "Paddle up, paddle up." We paddle the slave driver to his destination. When we get close enough to them, he calls out to their steersman, "oh, you guys need help, or you okay?"

"We good." He yells back, and points on the side with the 'ama. "Shmall kine pee break."

"Brah, bettah watch, get one tiger running loose—buggah was trying fo' eat my numbah five oh hea."

"Ho, nah," the steersman cooes and leans over the 'ama. "Braddah said get one tiger in da water."

"Minah." The voice says.

"How big was?" The other steersman asks.

The boys in front of us are stretching their arms across, trying to measure, but Ikaika answers, "like seventeen feet."

"How big?" the voice in the water yells.

"Seventeen."

"Seven?"

"Brah. Clean yo' ears. Seven-TEEN." The steersman shouts, and then whoop, the guy flies back in the boat.

"For real kine, cuz?"

"Ho, yeah." Ikaika answers. "Frickah oh hea was swimming beside it like one mermaid." I can feel him pointing at me.

"Yeah and fricka oh hea was chumming da watah so da t'ing can come by us." Their number two laughs.

"Brah, shut up." The guy that was in the water snaps. "I was urinating. It was urine."

Number two is cracking up. "Who pisses fo' dat long?"

"Brah, shut up." He says again. "So what, you guys like race, oh what?" The water guy bellows.

"Shoots!" Everyone in the boat except me answers.

"So from hea to da buoy way out dea." The steersman calls. "Kay, line 'em up, line 'em up."

We line up so that our canoes are as close to being nose and nose as possible. "Gabe, remembah just follow. Timing is erryt'ing. An' no just dip yo' paddle, put 'em all da way in 'til you wet your hand an' den pull up to da middle of yo' thigh. So reach out to da seat in front of you, and pull back to yo' thigh. Kay?"

I nod. I can remember that.

"You ready?" The other steersman asks. We all nod. Ikaika says, "you call."

"Shoot." The other guy answers. "Paddle up... hit."

Weird. So different from what Ikaika said earlier, but we're going with it. *Hut— ho*. I aim for the seat in front of me, sit up, pull hard until my paddle is parallel to my lap, release. Hut—

ho. We're picking up speed, and I can hear them right next to us *Hut—ho.*

"Power tens, next change." Ikaika says quietly, "pass it up."

"Power tens, next change!" I yell.

"Power ten, next change." The steersman in the boat next to us calls to his crew.

Joe-Joe's head snaps around and the look on his face says it all. That change was a secret. "One, two, three, four," he's counting loud enough so I can hear and I'm pulling as hard as I can as each number goes by. *Hut— ho.* "Again." He says, but this time I'm counting for myself. *Hut— ho.*

"Pick up the pace," Ikaika calls up, but this time I'm not saying anything. No one's going to shoot the messenger a dirty look this time. Somehow they hear him and we're all stroking faster. *Hut— ho.*

"Almost there, almost there." Georgie calls *like we can't see it.* "Push, push." Everyone's paddling as hard as we can. "All the way through, boys."

We paddle so hard I think my paddle's going to snap and my arms are going to come off until finally, we're through. We pass the buoy.

"Paddles up," Ikaika yells and we look next to us. There's no one there. We look behind and there they are, inching along. "Good race, good race." Our steersman calls to their steersman. Everyone in our boat is happy— including me. My first race, and we won.

We turn around and leave the other guys be, and start paddling back to where we came from. "Are we going in yet?" I ask. My mouth is dry and I am so winded.

"Shaddup." Ikaika replies. "Long run today. You need da practice."

"Practice for what?" I ask. Technically, I'm not even part of a team yet. This is my first time in a big boat.

"For da MacFarlane." Ikaika answers. "What you t'ink boys? We going take Gabe?"

"Hell yeah," comes their collective reply.

"When is it?" I wonder aloud.

"Next weekend—fourth of July." Uncle Nalu answers and makes his eyebrows dance.

I guess I'm part of a team now.

TWENTY FOUR

Uncle Nalu drops me off at home while everyone else is still at camp because, according to him, Mom told him she'd be home yesterday. "Brah, if dey did to you what I t'ink they went do, you're welcome to stay wit' me." He says, as we pull into the driveway. He parks right in front of the carport and opens his door.

Thanks but no thanks. Grandpa said that place is mine and if they don't come back, that's where I'm staying. "Sure." I tell him, and force a smile to form on my face. I roll myself out of the car, and am shocked by the amount of pain I feel in my butt and in my thighs. For a sport that looks like it's all arms, it sure hurts all over.

"I'll be right here, washing my car." He says, gripping the water hose.

"Yeah." I say, fart bag in hand, and run off down the trail that leads to *my* house. I knock on the door first, *like anyone's going to answer* and then let myself in. The house is just as I left it. A little messy, and stagnant. I open windows to let in the air and pick up the things I left lying around. "Mom," I call, *I hate being alone*, "Dad? Are you here?"

Just like always, I am greeted by air.

I take my things to the laundry room and toss them in there. Then I take my clothes off and dump them in the washer and start it up. I figure, it's about time. Then I run, naked to my bathroom—hand over my privates—so I can take a shower. Ice water turns to lobster boiling temperature and because it's either or and not both, I get out of there quickly and sit around on my bed.

There is nothing to do.

I roam the house. Go through my parent's room. They still have clothes hanging in their clothes, so maybe they didn't abandon me after all… then I hang out in Makena's room. She has a lot to do, a lot to look at, so I go through all of it. Her picture albums, her jewelry box which is filled with cheap rings that turned her fingers green and about a million best friend necklaces. A lot of people liked her. But who could blame them? She may have been evil but she was always laughing, always singing, always trying to be different. When I run out of things to look at, I remember the box I kicked under her bed. I reach underneath and pull it out.

My heart is beating because I know whatever she put in here must be really good secrets, unlike her journal that was filled with what she watched on TV when she was twelve, and which boy in her class had the neatest color hair. I pull the lid off and find slips of paper with quotes on it. Quotes by people like Audrey Hepburn, *"nothing is impossible. The word itself says 'I'm possible.'"* And Queen Lili‘uokalani, *"Onipa‘a"*

There are a few fortune cookie fortunes, and at the bottom, I find four sealed envelopes. The first one says: MOM, the second one reads: DAD, the third says: TO BE OPENED IN TEN YEARS, and the last one reads: GABE.

I put the box on the side, and open the one with my name on it. It's dated: 2013, which means she wrote it recently. I read:

Dear Gabriel,

If you are reading this, it means you are finally getting married. I never knew this day would actually happen because, well, look at you. You have a butt for a face. But I guess your wife/husband/dog/thing must really like butts because on top of looking like one, you smell and act like one too.

I stop reading, and laugh through the water that is dropping out of my eyes.

You know I'm just kidding right?

Duh.

So here's the deal. I actually like you Gabe, but you better not go around bragging about it or I'm going to punch you. Seriously punch you right in the face.

You know, I used to dream about having an older brother and a twin sister

Little did she know

But I never wished I didn't have you, my
baby brother. I know I said I wished you would die
a couple of times, but you know I never meant it
right? Even though you were such a pain it was just
you and me and I can honestly say that I never
wanted to trade you in

Gee, thanks, sis.

I hope at the time you are reading this you
found some success, doing I don't know what it
is that you like to do, robbing banks? Scrubbing
toilets? Who knows what you're up to by now, I don't
know because I'm not psychic but I hope you're
~~making lots of cash~~ happy.
You can do anything but being happy is
something you have to work on. Seriously, you're
smart, and responsible, and caring, and kind but
you have to learn to make yourself happy. You are
always there for me, I mean, I can't always count on
Mom and Dad, but I know I can always count on you.
You know, you're the reason I decided to stop
partying. I didn't like seeing the disappointment in
your eyes when I'd walk into the house late at night.
I didn't like how you'd take the fall for me when I
was stupid just so I wouldn't look like the bad guy.
I see you wanting good things for me, and it
makes me want good things for myself. I see you as

a friend, as someone who always wants good things for me even if you get mad and say you hate me. By the way: I forgive you.

I have to stop reading but my dripping eyes won't turn away.

I'm not going to get all mushy and stuff but I hope you know that I do love you very much. I don't have much advice to give you because like I said earlier, you're a pretty smart kid, but I will say this: stop being so serious. Don't throw your life away by not doing your best. Live big, make memories, and take care of yourself. Stop trying to take care of everyone else. Mom, Dad and me? We can handle it. We got this. Stop taking care of us and start taking care of you and your new family.

So anyway, I wish you and your new whatever all the love and happiness in the world. I hope you fill your house with crying, screaming, loud, obnoxious voices and that you'll consider naming one (or maybe all) of them after me.

> With so much sweetness and crap that I'm seriously going to barf if I don't end this,
>> Makena

"What are you doing?" Mom's voice makes me jump so high I fall off the bed.

I didn't even hear them come home. "Nothing," I stuff the letter back into the envelope.

"Give it to me." She says, holding out her hand. I notice fresh red paint atop fake, sharpened nails.

I shake my head. "It's mine."

"Give it to me. NOW."

"No," I'm raising my voice because there is just no way she's taking this letter away from me. "This is mine. Makena wrote this for me."

"Why would she write something to you?"

"She wrote a letter to all of us." I say, trying to sound reasonable. "Here's yours, and here's Dad's."

Mom stomps into the room and grabs everything off the bed. She flips the envelopes marked, 'MOM' and 'DAD' around in her hand, and then puts it in the box. "Now hand it over." She growls, and holds her hand out again.

I move away from her as fast as I can and run for the front door.

"Gavin, stop him!" She shrieks, and Dad wheels himself over and blocks me in.

"Whoa, what you got there, buddy?" He drawls.

"Nothing for you." I spit.

"It's Makena's." Mom cries.

"It's mine." I whine.

"Let's see it." Dad croons.

I can hear Uncle Nalu's stereo playing and wonder if he'd be able to hear me through it. Mom's getting closer, so I try out my lungs. "Nalu, help!"

"Nalu, help." Mom laughs and tries snatching my letter

away.

"What's your problem?" I ask her. "I already told you that it's mine, Makena wrote it to me so why are you trying to take it away?"

"Because it's mine." She crows, and tries grabbing at it again.

"What makes it yours?" I want to know. I need to know why she's acting like this.

"Because it belongs to Makena."

"And everything that belongs to Makena belongs to you?" I ask.

"Yes, it does, now give it here." Mom's snarling; she doesn't even look like my mother anymore.

"Mom," I cry as she yanks it out of my hands, "it's mine, it's mine, it's mine." I watch her greedy eyes eat through the words—the words that were supposed to be mine and my future whatever's. She finishes reading, folds it up, puts it back in it's envelope and sticks it in the box. This ticks me off. "What makes her so special?"

"Oh, shut up." She snaps.

"No, Mom. I want to know. What makes Makena so much more special than me? Than Nalu?"

"Don't—" she grimaces. "Don't bring Uncle Nalu into this, he's got nothing to do with nothing."

"He's got everything to do with everything." I wail, "why did you choose her over him? And why are you choosing her over me?"

"What are you even talking—you don't know what you're talking about." Mom is stammering, her brown eyes looking for an answer everywhere else.

"Mom," I cry, "they told me everything. I know everything. I know that Nalu is my brother. That he and Makena are Ikaika's."

"Makena is your father's!" Mom shrieks.

I pretend I don't hear her and go on. "That you changed your name so you could run away. That U'i is my sister."

"How is U'i your sister?" She screams.

"Through Dad." I tell her.

"How dare you," Mom is yelling, "how dare you say that to me—you can accuse me of many things Gabe but don't you dare accuse your Dad."

"Don't accuse him of what? Being someone else's father? Why not? It's true. Everyone knows it. And it makes sense to me why they were flirting outside the other day…" I said too much. Mom is grabbing the box and the jar of ashes and heading back to her bedroom.

Dad is looking at me with pure hate streaming out of his eyes. I blink but by the time I open my eyes, he launches himself at me—just jumps up out of his wheelchair and grabs me. "Listen, punk. Mom and I are going through some stuff that you would never know. We're going through some stuff that you would never imagine."

I push him off of me and he falls back into his chair. "I'm going through the same things as you Dad. I'm going through the *exact* same thing as the both of you. I lost Makena too, I lost a friend and a sister and a Mom and a Dad so how *dare* you say that I don't know what you are going through. I know what you're going through only *I'm going through it by myself.* Dad,

211

Mom. At least you have each other. I have no one.

When we first got here I hated it. Nobody cared about what I'm going through, nobody wanted me to be myself, *everyone* wanted me to conform; to be something I am not, and no, I'm not perfect, but at least I can say I tried. I tried to fit in even when nobody wanted me there. You—you and Mom— you don't even try. You don't even want to get along, all you do is run away. Run away from your problems, run away from your mistakes, run away from me. All you do is think about yourselves and I hate it. I hate that you choose to love and take care of a dead, plastic bottle more than you love and take care of me." I look at the front door and he moves away. I take that as my exit stage left, so I grab the handle. "I'm going where someone loves me, like you care."

I run up the driveway and notice that the baby hawks are flying, and that one of seems to be leading me straight to Nalu's house. I take that as a sign, and follow it like Grandma said our ancestors did oh so long ago.

TWENTY FIVE

I didn't go back. Not even to get my clothes because I didn't want to have anything to do with them. And I guess they didn't want to have anything to do with me either because neither of them bothered to come over. Not that I'd know what I'd say if they did. I'm over apologies; there was I time when I expected them, maybe because I thought I deserved them, or maybe because I thought that they cared for me as much as I cared about them but now, I don't want them. I don't want anything. Let them keep Makena, let them grow old on the memory of her ashes for all eternity. Me, I'd rather spend my time living.

Today is the big day, the day of the race and right now, it's three in the morning and we're trailering the ugliest outrigger canoe in our little fleet to Waikiki where the race is. I guess this one is a big deal— you have to be invited in order to race it and because the area they give us to race on is so small, not everyone gets an invitation. Lucky for me we got in purely because of how my cousins and their team have been doing so far this season, and the team must have felt sorry for me because they're letting me jump in to seat five for this race they call the MacFarlane race.

(And no, it's not named after the MacFarlane Queen Liliʻuokalani mentioned in her book. The race is named after the guy who was once the president of Outrigger Canoe Club, Walter MacFarlane.) According to Mirry, 'it's the most funnest race in the world,' and it takes place on the part of the beach people call, 'Duke's Beach' after Olympic gold medalist and father of the 'Kahanamoku kick,' Duke Kahanamoku.

Today they say waves are supposed to be five feet and even though we've been practicing wave surfing in the canoe I'm nervous because here, they measure waves by the backs of it, not by the faces like they do back in Cali. But I'm trying to keep cool, especially since Napua's with me. We're sitting in the bed of Uncle Nalu's pickup truck (as usual) but this time I don't mind— even though Napua's hair is smacking the beard *I'm going to have one day* off of my face and even though the bumps in the freeway are big enough to toss us around, and even though all we do is read books next to each other and touch hands every now and then, it's okay. Napua is my girl now. *Deanna who?*

Every now and then she'll grab my muscular *what? One day they will be* arms and smile at me, her face so close I want to lean in and kiss it, but I don't. Maybe one day soon, but it definitely has to happen.

As we pull into the alley to unload our canoe, I can't stop noticing how tourist ridden Waikiki is. Everything here is fake— fake flower leis hanging from fake tikis, fake coconut cups sitting on fake 'wooden' trays, but the people here—even at four in the morning—are eating it up and I like it. I like the smell of fake coconut in the air, the sound of the waves hitting the shore deep and low like drums and cymbals.

Uncle stops the truck and the security guard tells us to hurry up. We get out and a bunch of adults who are part of our club, and a bunch who are a part of other clubs run around and help. They take the straps off and help us slide the canoe off of the trailer. Everyone's smiling and laughing and joking around; it's really weird. We walk it down the long alley and toward the beach—which, strange as it sounds is a lot easier than I described it because there are so many people helping that it's like we're really all just carrying a plate. "Ovah dea," one of the guys from the club yells and we walk it to the left, and leave it for the adults to put the canoe together.

U'i comes over and drags Napua away from me, so I'm alone again. The old me would have sat around moping, but today, I'm getting in there. I'm helping them set up, I'm watching them rig. This part is like a puzzle, the ropes have to go up and under and over and through some holes; I'm dizzy trying to figure it out and then they pull on it tightly so the 'ama won't detach from the boat.

Little by little the light starts getting brighter and brighter and the surf shows itself in the sunlight. My heart jumps. *So this is what it's like. This is the race that Mom did when she met Dad.* I wonder about the two of them, wonder what they're doing, wonder if they know we're here.

Someone brings me a donut and I chomp on it, and then I feast on two more while we're waiting for this regatta to start. There are hundreds of people filling the beach—so many people you can barely find sand to sit on—and I'm getting the same kind of nervous I got that day I escaped the mouth of that shark. An announcer starts talking over the squealing PA system and after announcing that the race is going to start, someone blows a low horn like instrument.

I find Mirry standing under the shade of the tent and tap her on her arm. "That sounds pretty. What is that? One of those nose flute things?"

Mirry rolls her eyes at me and puts her hands on her hips. "No, that's a pū."

"What's a pū?" I ask. Nevermind her sass, one day when she's older I'll deal with it but like Aunty Jo said, she's young and dumb and I really want to know.

"A conch shell." She says, and then holds her arms out for someone behind me. "Mommy, you're here."

Aunty Vai sees me and smiles for the first time since I've met her.

The races are starting, and Grandma and Grandpa still aren't around. I'm getting worried because it's my first actual race and I want them to see me—especially since I know my parents won't be there. The boats go in and all the little kids—Mirry included—get in the boat and ready themselves to paddle.

I look around for Napua, I wish she were here next to me. She calms me. Takes my mind off of my fears. I can't find her.

"Gabe." Joe-Joe is calling, "Come stand ovah hea. We going out soon."

Oh God I'm going to throw up. My paddle, whose got my paddle?

Napua comes out of nowhere and hands me my paddle. "Go get 'em babe."

Babe?

"Thanks," I say and smile so big I can't see anything

216

anymore. Great. I turned into U'i. The boats are racing back in and a new batch of kids is getting ready to go out. *These waves are big.* "When are we going in?" I ask Joe-Joe.

"You folks are up next," it's Grandpa. My grandparents are here. Finally, I can breathe. I have so much nervous energy I'm jumping up and down. "Who's steering?" Grandpa's asking Uncle Nalu. "You, or Ikaika?"

Uncle Nalu looks thoughtful, and then moves to the side. Mom. What's she doing here? "Haunani going steer."

"You sure?" Grandpa's eyebrows are raised.

She nods.

Grandpa is not convinced. "But you haven't been in da boat for ages." He takes off his hat, and scratches his head. "You remebah how, oh what?"

"Yes." She says, quietly.

"Da waves are big. I don't know."

Ikaika jumps in. "Let her steer. Trust me. Just let her go."

"Okay," Grandpa sighs. "Up to you, but if you break my boat,"

"No worries pops." Uncle Nalu laughs. "She get 'em, She get 'em. Can."

The boats are coming in. One of them flips over, and all the kids are tossed out like the trash on garbage day. "Dass one sign, look." Grandpa cries.

"Dad." Mom says, and looks up into Grandpa's eyes. "I can do it."

A softness washes over his face for a brief moment and he shakes his head. "You right Haunani. You right."

Our boat is in and everyone's running to jump into it.

The waves are washing in and the boat is rocking up and down making it impossible to get in it. *Am I the only one having a hard time?* I look around. *Yes, I am.* Even Mom is in the boat. *I'm such a wuss.*

I pull as hard as I can and just as I'm jumping up, a wave pushes me right into the boat. I scramble to get into seat five, and Mom's calling, "ho'omau-kau-kau, e kau-pe, pā!"

Our paddles hit the water and we pull as hard as we can. It's no easy task because the tide is fighting against us, and the waves are trying to jump in and take a ride too but we manage to paddle way out to the flags where everyone is lining up. "Bail." Mom says, and Georgie grabs the bleach bottle that was cut to make a scooper and starts shoveling water out of the boat. "Lining up," Mom shouts, and we paddle forward. "Back paddle, back paddle," Mom instructs and everyone turns their paddles over—advertisement facing us, and we all paddle backwards in sync. "Watch the flag." Mom yells.

We all get into starting position, which is leaning forward with our paddles just above the water. The guy holding the red flag puts it into a holder in his boat and grabs two more flags—a yellow and a green one. He holds the yellow flag, and drops it fast while bringing up the green with his other hand. "Go, go, go!" Mom screams, and we dig as hard as we can.

We are flying, the waves are pushing us from behind and crashing over themselves in front. We go over one wave and the water throws itself all over seat one and seat two. Joe-Joe and John are leaning back with their paddles in the air but the rest of us are paddling as hard as we can. I see the 'ama pop up and I'm so scared we're going to fall in like the last group of people but

218

I can feel Mom jumping up and down behind me. *What is she doing?* I want to look but I'm not going to.

We near the shore and people are just screaming for us as loud as they can. We reach the flags and Mom yells, "paddles up." I turn to look both ways as if I'm crossing the street, first left, then right and see that there's no one next to us. We won. WE WON.

We paddle to shore slowly, ride a swell in, and when we reach the guys who are waiting for our canoe to come in, we spill out of the boat. Everyone is congratulating us— there are people are taking pictures, and a tunnel that leads us up the beach that stretches as far as the street. We run through and people are patting me on the back, rubbing my head, yelling, 'good job!' When we get to the end, I see Dad sitting there with Makena's bottle. He reaches up to hug me and I lean down to him, but then he surprises me and stands. I stop, and he takes a few tentative steps forward towards me. I start to cry—I was a kid the last time I saw him walk.

He reaches out again, and I hug him. Not a hard, crashing hug, but a soft I'm proud of you hug.

"Love you son." He whispers in my ear.

"Love you too, Dad." I wail. I am such a wuss.

"We're uh, we're setting Makena out to sea today."

I'm in shock. I don't know what he means. Are they going to take her bottle and float her away? "No. You can't." I say, finally.

"We have to." He says, his lips drawing themselves into a thin line. "It was-- you know, it was in those letters you found. She wanted it this way."

"What do you mean?" I think he's gone nuts.

Mom finally exits the tunnel and drapes her arm around my shoulder. "Did Dad tell you?" She asks me.

"Yeah." I shrug.

"So we're thinking about naming it Makena if it's a girl. Would that be weird?"

I have no clue what she's talking about. "Mom? You're going to name the jar Makena and set it out to sea?"

"What? No. We're having a baby."

I can't believe it. They're so old. Gross.

She sees my face and then laughs. "Oh. He told you about the ceremony. After this race is done, a bunch of the clubs here are going to come out with us and scatter your sister's ashes out at sea. We talked a lot about what you said, about how we focus more on her ashes than we do on you, more on her death than we do on our lives. You were right." She reaches into her bag, which is on the arm of Dad's wheelchair and pulls out the letter. "I'm giving this back to you. It's yours. I had no right to take it. But

I'm going to keep it in here so you don't lose it, okay?"

I nod. "Thanks Mom." I say, and let her hug me.

From the corner of my eye, I see Napua. I reach out for her and she folds herself into my arms and holds me. Things will never be perfect, but with Napua in my arms, and my family all around me, I think I'm going to be okay.

Multi-ethnic (Kanaka Maoli / Asian / Apache/ Caucasian) writer
MONICA K.K. LEE is the author of a poetry book, and a novel. Her
short stories and poetry have been published in several
literary journals. She was born and raised on O'ahu where she
graduated with her BA in English. She lives, breathes, and
paddles outrigger canoes in Hawai'i with her soulmate and their kiddos.

43997281R00142

Made in the USA
Lexington, KY
19 August 2015